Prai

LEADERSHIP IS OVERCOMING THE NATURAL

"The special sauce to creating a high-performance and caring leadership culture is in this book. Joe Judge and Michael D. Merrill have assembled a greatest hits list of management-enhancing approaches for both experienced and aspiring executives. If you're committed to strengthening your own personal toolbox and developing more well-rounded future leaders around you, there isn't a better roadmap than following these 52 maxims."

Frank Hugelmeyer, President & CEO, National Marine Manufacturers Association

"*Leadership Is Overcoming the Natural* reminds me of the flight attendant before takeoff who instructs passengers that in a moment of turbulence, please first secure your oxygen mask, before attempting to assist others. The same rules apply to leadership. So often society pushes the 'till the wheels fall off' mentality, but doesn't warn you of the aftermath of when the wheels *really* fall off (i.e., health issues, divorce, toxic atmosphere, failed leadership, bankruptcy, etc.). The book guides you on how to harness and leverage the natural power of taking care of your mental, physical, and spiritual well-being, before attempting to 'lead' others."

Joshua Reid, CEO & Founder, Inphlu, Inc.

"In this clear and concise work, Judge and Merrill condense their years of experience, wisdom and passion for service into an innovative framework for leadership that will greatly enhance the success of any team. All great leaders care about their teams and the people they serve, but by reframing how leaders need to demonstrate that care in a series of clear, actionable steps, they've created a counter-intuitive but powerful new tool to maximize every leader's potential for success."

John A. Vaughn, MD, Assistant Vice President for Student Affairs & Student Health Director, Associate Professor, Family Medicine & Community Health, Duke University

"*Leadership Is Overcoming the Natural* offers forward and practical leadership advice on how to rise above your natural instincts and inclinations to become your true best self. Whether you are currently a leader or aspire to become one, this book will help you take charge of your own leadership development to advance your team and organization positively forward."

Lisa D. Shreve, MPP, Senior Vice President of Professional Education, AHIP

"Most leadership books are dreadfully predictable. Many are written from the ivory tower of good ideas. This one's the exception. Judge and Merrill deliver the face punch that forces us to get real with ourselves for the first time."

Casey Graham, CEO and Co-founder, Gravy

"For the past twenty-plus years, I've watched Joe Judge coach leaders at all levels of an organization on the maxims detailed in this book. These principles work, plain and simple! I've seen the success firsthand for those who embrace Joe's teachings; these are life changing tools for leaders."

Jennifer Schultz, Human Relations Director, Desert Research Institute

"I found this book to be one of the most contemporary and relevant leadership reads in existence. Every leader, regardless of their job title, should own a copy of this book, like Christians own the Bible. For those who are seriously interested in and committed to success, the 52 maxims are a *must-read* into how they carry themselves professionally and personally."

Darrell "Flash" Gordon, CEO, Wernle Youth and Family Treatment Center and author of *Change Does Not Occur in a Flash*

"Drawing on the years of experience Mike and Joe have amassed in healthcare and other industries, these maxims get right to the real issues and opportunities leaders face with practical examples to provide context for the reader that makes these lessons actionable."

Michael Cropp, MD, CEO, Independent Health, Buffalo, NY

"The authors provide an engaging, thought-provoking journey that guides the reader with real-life experiences and practical tips on how to become a transformational leader. A must-read for anyone looking to lead a successful team."

Craig Kirby, CEO, Recreational Vehicle Industry Association (RVIA)

"Joe and Mike have summed up leadership principles in this book that work, plain and simple. I am a student of Joe's teachings and believe that Joe's purpose is to develop the character of a leader. Joe's life examples have positively influenced Whataburger's culture and success for two decades and counting. Joe and Mike provide a framework that will change your life as a leader of people."

Ed Nelson, President and CEO, Whataburger

LEADERSHIP *is* OVERCOMING *the* NATURAL

52 MAXIMS TO MOVE BEYOND INSTINCT

JOE JUDGE · MICHAEL MERRILL

Advantage®

Published by Advantage, Charleston, South Carolina.
Member of Advantage Media Group.

Printed in the United States of America.

10 9 8 7 6 5 4 3 2 1

ISBN: 978-1-64225-350-4
LCCN: 2022907543

Cover design by Hampton Lamoureux.
Layout design by Wesley Strickland.

This book is dedicated to our families. For Joe, this is his wife Theresa; his kids Heather and her husband Charlie, Bryan and his wife Jessie, and Kelley and her husband Joe; and his grandkids, Charlotte, Fallon, Dalton, Jack, and Porter. For Mike, this is his wife Melanie, and his kids Michael and Maeanna.

CONTENTS

PREFACE BY JOE JUDGE

Three years ago, I decided to grab a quick breakfast before a session with sixty executives I had never met. I selected a table and soon found myself engaged in a pleasant conversation with Dr. Michael Merrill. Little did I know Mike and I would not only become friends but that together we would write a book.

After the session Mike reached out and said, "Let's take these ideas and write a book."

I responded, "Thank you, but I am going to let you down." For years I had wondered about writing a book, but each time my insecurities got the best of me, and I would wind up hitting the pause button. Several times, people I met along the way offered to help, but I never felt I could accept.

But Mike wouldn't take no for an answer. Finally, he said, "Look, all you have to do is talk. I'll write down what you say, rewrite it, and together we'll make this work." For some reason I said yes. What I have found is that through Mike's encouragement, intelligence, and writing experience, we somehow stayed the course. While Mike is a highly gifted writer, doctor, and student, I am a hacker trying to figure out what works and what doesn't.

Some have described me as a "beggar showing other beggars where to find bread." That description captures my style and mindset better than any other description. My life has been a quest to learn those things I don't know and share them with others who are also searching. This journey has placed me amid brilliant, highly successful individuals who are always striving to get better.

In these pages, you will find a summary of what Mike and I have learned as patterns emerged. While not everything here will be of value to every reader, our hope is that you find something that supports your own journey toward better leadership.

Introduction

GREAT LEADERSHIP IS NOT NATURAL

When we try to encapsulate leadership in a word like "influence," there's always something we omit.

Leadership is a human process that changes, is complex, and is more complicated than simple definitions can fully describe. Definitions are mere signs pointing toward the larger goal of leadership, but they do not summarize leadership itself. And at some point, definitions can't help but get in the way. For this reason, we must be ready to discard them when they fall short.

There's an old image from Zen literature of a finger pointing at the moon. The finger isn't important. The important point of emphasis, as it relates to leadership, is the moon. It's large, mysterious, and far away. We can point at leadership, but we can't put it in a box.

Likewise, nothing that happens to you, or anything you do, will make you into a true leader. Getting a promotion or taking specific coursework is not enough. Even reading this book will not turn you into a leader, though we hope it will guide you in the right direction.

The reason for this is that leadership is not natural.

Leadership Is Overcoming the Natural

In our natural state, if someone attacks us, we get defensive. If someone hurts our feelings, we disengage. If conflict is foreign to us, we avoid it. If someone questions us, we act insulted. If someone thinks differently than we do, it's easy to avoid them. If someone makes us extremely angry, we yell in retaliation.

All these responses feel natural and good, even though they can result in horrible consequences for individuals and organizations.

But to become excellent leaders, we must be aware of traits within ourselves and the actions we take that are detrimental to others. We must work on changing ourselves into someone better. This takes a lot of practice, but eventually it pays off.

When we focus on improving our actions and responses, it's as though we become a new person that rises to a higher level of behavior. In time, this fresh pattern becomes the new natural.

Commit to Self-Reflection

At this point, our new natural self should become subject to our ongoing reflection. As we look further, we will see a new set of suboptimal traits and behaviors. There are still things about us that are not good for ourselves, our group, and our organization. The new natural is now something to be overcome, as we work to become a better person.

This path is a journey of self-reflection, which is not always easy. One way to strengthen your commitment is to journal. Whether you choose to use a digital journal or the old pen-and-paper method is up to you. But we would encourage you to start. Begin by describing not just what happened today but the reasons you chose a certain thought or action.

Examining your responses gives you the opportunity to better identify thoughts, behaviors, and reactions to use the next time a similar situation arises. When you recognize a response, situation, or feeling you have seen before, this is a time to pause and ask yourself what needs to change. Journaling is structured reflection time. Because leaders often fail to receive valid, candid feedback, these times are critical self-evaluation moments.

Another way to gain insight and pursue thoughtful action is to share with a few close team members the areas that you are working on changing and to invite them to help you. Some thoughts and behaviors are easy to change, but others will be a struggle. When we struggle, we need help. Those trusted team members, when they see the behavior you are trying to change, can remind you. That feedback—unwelcome as it may feel at times—is invaluable.

Most important, challenge yourself to go beyond your natural, learned tendencies. Just because something *feels* right does not mean it *is* right. Some things that feel natural are not necessarily good.

There's been a theme in American culture for years that can be summarized with a few statements:

- "Work smarter, not harder."
- "If it hurts, you overdid it."
- "Don't let them see you sweat."

Unfortunately, these aphorisms suggest that if something is hard it must be wrong. But sometimes hard is just what we need to break out of the natural. It was Maya Angelou who said, "Do the best you can until you know better. Then when you know better, do better." She is right, and this is what real leadership is all about.

Because great leadership is not natural, you must be comfortable with the unnatural to become the leader others want to follow.

Sometimes Our Natural Instincts Are Wrong

When I first became a leader of a small group of physicians and nurse practitioners, I knew I had something to learn about leadership, but that didn't keep me from making mistakes. I tried behaving naturally, and it didn't always work.

One day, eating lunch in the cafeteria with two of my employees, I offered one of them some negative feedback. I had been worried about a particular issue for days, and I took the opportunity to articulate my concerns. As I spoke, my employee held her poker face, but later when we were alone, she blew up at me. She was angry I confronted her in front of her coworker. And the more I thought about her response, the more I realized she was right. I had made the wrong call. That conversation should have taken place somewhere between just the two of us.

That day, I learned my instincts had to be carefully examined. My intention was good, but that didn't promise the best outcome. I was scared, and when I'm scared, I come across as arrogant. This makes no sense to me, but it's true. When I'm most nervous, I give off a strong sense that I am still in control, and I can easily become awkward and foolish.

–Mike

Moving Beyond the Natural

Step 1: List some of the leadership myths you have discovered and note some of the ways leadership has expanded your comfort zone.

Step 2: Create a journal and commit to self-reflection for one month.

Step 3: Ask one person on your team you respect and trust to provide you with one way you could improve your leadership communication.

Notes

Maxim 1

LEADERSHIP IS A DECISION—MAKE SURE YOU'RE READY

Leadership is not a job title. It's not even a role we play. Real leadership is a decision to move into a specific relationship with others. In this relationship, it's the leader's responsibility to move people and organizations into the future, adding value to both in the process. Now you're not just part of a team. You have responsibility for people and their futures.

Too few people understand the depth of their decision to become a leader. They fail to comprehend that when you enter this form of relationship, you can't just do what feels right or easy. You must do the whole job. Much of it is hard, and it challenges you to examine your assumptions and be open to rethinking the truths you thought you knew.

Remember, doing something hard doesn't mean it is wrong. Sometimes, good results require hard work.

Question to Ask Before You Lead

Before you enter a new leadership position, there are several steps of self-evaluation you should go through to check if you are ready.

CHECK 1: WHY DO I WANT TO BE A LEADER?

Before accepting a position as a leader, ask yourself why you want it. The answer should be something like, "Because I love serving, developing, and helping people achieve their dreams."

If your answer lands in a different ballpark, think twice.

Leadership is not about power or position. Leadership is not about being served or having instant respect. Leadership has many unpleasant moments. There will be sleepless nights as you prepare to dismiss someone who does not fit the organization. There will be days of anxiety as you choose between two strategies when you only have the resources for one. On many days, your fears and insecurities will surface, and yet you will have to continue, because others are counting on you.

Given these downsides, any motive other than serving people will be inadequate.

CHECK 2: AM I WILLING TO GROW INTO THE POSITION?

You need to know what leadership skills you have and where you need improvement. You must be willing to work on your weak spots. If you don't, you run the risk of doing harm to yourself, your team, and your organization. Even worse, you'll send a message to people around you that self-development is not important.

The list of leadership qualities is classic and doesn't change much with time. If you do not know where to start, Korn Ferry has a great list of thirty-eight competencies that will give you some perspective of your strengths and weaknesses. No one does all of them well, but take an inventory. Ask others for feedback. And after that, decide if you are willing to lean into your strengths and improve those areas where you are weak.

The old *Are leaders born or made?* debate is irrelevant to this point. True leaders are both born and made, with every one of them having high and low points. It is critical to cultivate leadership skills, but of even greater importance is the willingness to stretch, grow, and develop.

CHECK 3: AM I WILLING TO BE UNCOMFORTABLE?

Leadership is not comfortable for anyone. Yes, there are times when everything runs smoothly, but at other points it is messy. It involves moving people into the future and means you and your team are constantly in transition, working with the unknown and the unproven.

This can create anxiety and raises the question: How comfortable are you being uncomfortable? Do you avoid discomfort and shut down, or does it energize you to bring out your creative side and be at your best?

It is possible to be comfortable being uncomfortable, but doing so requires much intentionality and practice.

Breaking the Glass Ceiling of Discomfort

Catherine faced an uphill leadership challenge. She was part of a manufacturing organization where the glass ceiling for women was an obvious barrier to her career advancement.

It was not until the CEO retired, and a new one came on board, that the ceiling was raised. Catherine was promoted to SVP and placed over a large HR department. Her list of qualifications was lengthy.

She had the ability to bring people together, listen, and solve problems. However, she lacked experience in HR. Knowing this, she did something that was essential to her team's success. She gathered a group of twelve individuals from the HR department and six members of the executive team. During a daylong meeting, they outlined current issues and obstacles in a way that made the HR leaders feel heard and understood. They detailed the costs to the business, both financial and emotional, in the current way that HR was being run.

Next, they excused the executives and moved into a room with four walls of whiteboards. The team was asked to reconstruct HR, while meeting needs, removing obstacles, and creating accountabilities.

Catherine trusted the team to find solutions, and over the next six months HR was transformed into a highly effective asset of the organization and a source of strategic problem-solving. At the same time, the limits that had previously been put on women in that organization were abolished. Today, the executive team is now not only half women but continues to strive to add new and different lenses as they grow.

Catherine was placed in a role that no other female in her company had ever experienced, and yet she was able to flourish because she grew into the position and leaned on those around her.

–Joe

Moving Beyond the Natural

Step 1: Ask yourself, *Why do I want to lead?*

Step 2: Evaluate how you have dealt with discomfort in the past. How do you handle change? How do you respond to pressure?

Step 3: Decide if you are willing to grow into your new role. Inevitably, there will be leadership situations you did not anticipate. But in those moments, are you willing to evolve, grow, and lean on those who can help?

Notes

Maxim 2

EVERY LEADER SHOULD HAVE A CABINET

Some leaders are made, and others are born, but every one of them needs help.

By the time you become an adult, you already have some, but probably not all, of the requirements of leadership. Even if you are lucky enough to have been born with or to have absorbed the basics, you still need to improve and learn.

Whatever we are born with and can learn is never the complete package. The lessons of leadership are as complex as humanity itself.

In past decades, the personality type of the hierarchical, military-style leader was dominant in the upper levels of business. This is no longer a requirement. As the business world evolves, we see increasing diversity in leadership styles and personalities. In fact, with the proliferation of technology companies, personality types such as Elon Musk—who do not give off the typical leadership vibe—now hold positions of authority.

No imperfection disqualifies you from being a leader, and no one is forbidden to lead. You can lead with any sort of mind, any sort of background, and any sort of emotional makeup. You can have any kind of disability and still be a leader.

The only requisites to being a leader are the willingness to challenge oneself and the desire to learn from others.

Four Cabinet Members Every Leader Needs

I (Joe) was once in a conversation with an individual who had built an international brand. What I remember most from that dialogue was one sentence: "If I were building a snow cone stand today, the first thing I'd do is hire a board of directors."

As individuals, when assessing the effect we have on others, it's easy to have a very narrow view. We judge ourselves based mostly on our intentions. But when we actually do something in the world, like market a product or give feedback to another person, others view us in a much wider context. They seldom consider our intentions. Instead, they only see our behavior, and they judge our behavior in the light of their own beliefs and experiences.

Sometimes, this might cause them to question our intent or disconnect from us. When we lack perspective, we have very little ability to predict the net effects of our behavior. Without people around to challenge us, offer feedback, question our strategies, and hold us accountable, we become the biggest threat to our own success.

One of the most helpful questions you can ask yourself is, *Who knows me well enough to always tell me the truth?* Who has been where I want to go, or has experience and insight to share? Who kicks my butt when I get stuck and helps me get over the obstacles that need to be confronted? Who holds me accountable to who I am, what I am doing, and why I am doing it? These special people can serve as your cabinet.

A cabinet should consist of the following people:

CABINET MEMBER 1: MENTORS

Look for people who have been where you want to go. These are generally individuals who have held high positions, have great influence, or are known for their wisdom and ability. A mentor is someone you trust to advise, challenge, and hold you accountable.

CABINET MEMBER 2: COACHES

These are individuals who know you well and challenge you to be better. You confide in such coaches at a level of intimacy and vulnerability. Based on their knowledge of your character, they know where you tend to step back, where you should be stepping forward, and where you step forward when you should be pausing. They help you navigate your fears and insecurities. They check in with those around you to make sure you have the information necessary to make progress.

CABINET MEMBER 3: FRIENDS

A true friend will get you without judgment and will believe in you no matter what. You can lean on them in hard seasons. They are not there to give you perfect advice, but they are there to lift your spirits and remind you of the person that you are.

CABINET MEMBER 4: FAMILY

Whether it is your blood family or a group of people close to you, no one knows you better. Your family is uniquely able to share thoughts and insights that no one else might ever share.

Your cabinet members don't have to sit down at a formal meeting and deliberate on your success. But keep a list of them and check in with them from time to time. Go to them with important decisions. Consult them when you are stuck. And reciprocate their generosity to you by helping them when you can.

The Value of Multiple Voices

Telling the truth is mercy. In medical training, it is invaluable.

I was fortunate enough to spend eight hours a week for five years doing outpatient training with a highly talented group of internists and family physicians. They knew and cared about me, so I received extensive feedback every day. This molded me to the point where now my thinking on medical problems is divided into the approaches of my various mentors from that clinic.

The voice of one doctor tells me to be very careful about interpreting the medical literature. The voice of another reminds me to be thorough and recheck my work over and over. And another voice tells me to have some fun and love my patients.

This is the value of having multiple members in my cabinet.

–Mike

Moving Beyond the Natural

Step 1: Write down the names of four people who can serve as your cabinet and fill each of the roles mentioned in this section.

Step 2: Set up a meeting with each of them and *formally* ask them to join your cabinet team.

Step 3: Commit to following up with these individuals every month for one year.

Notes

Maxim 3

PEOPLE FOLLOW THOSE WHO DEMONSTRATE EMOTIONAL AWARENESS

The workplace is not a computer. It is not a predictable machine that creates output according to logical rules that, if only created correctly, will be highly reliable and productive. We know this through experience.

Have you ever tried to introduce a group of people to a new standard operating procedure? If so, did they all embrace it? Likely not. Some people faced with change will actively or passively obstruct it. Every workplace consists of people who have a wide variety of emotional and philosophical differences.

To manage and lead these different personalities, you must have an awareness of that dimension of humanness. You must be aware of your own emotions and those of the people around you. Even more challenging, you must be aware of how those sets of emotions interact and flow in and out of a group.

If you do not do this and fail to account for the emotions of others in your decision-making process, your team will start to disengage. They will not function as well as they would otherwise, and you will be likely to fail.

As you become more aware of your own feelings, reactions, and fears, you will be much more equipped to lead people and relate to them. Introspection is the key to emotional awareness. Some of the people who are the best at this are psychologists and other psychotherapists.

During training, professionals study their own feelings about patients with guidance from a supervisor. These feelings then become important clues to the patient's status. It's as if they have learned to create data conduits from their instincts and intuitions into their conscious mind. You can do this too. Your emotions in the moment create important data about what is going on in the social space around you.

You Can Improve Any Situation

The danger to this way of living is becoming superstitious. Emotions that are not reflected on are not a reliable doorway to the truth, so don't fix on a specific interpretation of a strong emotion. Examining your emotions does not give you an excuse to stop thinking.

Rather, remember you have the power to improve your emotional intelligence. This only happens through focus and determination. The best leadership is intentional and does not come naturally. Just because you are good at a frontline job doesn't mean you'll be good at leading frontline people. Leadership is a separate skill set. Some people are naturally better at it than others, but whether you're a natural or not, you can improve.

As a leader, the instrument you bring to the workplace is yourself. Your ability to think and develop people, and get work done through people, will determine whether others recognize you as a leader. To be a better leader, you must understand and improve yourself. You must be emotionally aware.

Real leadership is not superficial. It is not a matter of deciding how to hold your pencil or pitch your voice in a meeting. It involves your emotions and past experiences, as well as your ability to be aware of yourself in a shifting, sometimes chaotic environment.

Learning about yourself involves reflection and feedback. These actions don't come naturally to most people, and this journey is sometimes painful. But know that through your pain, you can always improve and accurately assess your surroundings.

Be Aware of Your Leadership Capacity and Emotional Energy Levels

> In medicine, when you are with a very sick patient, this creates energy. And the amount of energy created can be overwhelming. It's important to do something with it. If you don't, you can panic. Generally, that means thinking intensely and acting with care and precision. The unifying principle pulling that energy together is service to the patient. Focusing that emotional energy on the human being, not the symptoms or the medications, can then lead to the best outcome.
>
> *–Mike*

An entrepreneur I used to work with developed a rapidly expanding business. When the company began to grow, the founder brought in a therapist to keep the relationships healthy, so the company didn't go off track. Then when the company hit $100 million in sales, he brought in a CEO, because he knew he couldn't handle the job anymore. This was brilliant leadership. Sometimes, becoming your better self involves knowing your limits and getting out of the way.

–Joe

Notes

Maxim 4

THE WAY YOU DO ONE THING IS THE WAY YOU DO EVERYTHING

Compartmentalization seldom works. Deep down, who you are in one space is who you are everywhere.

One step into somebody's car and you have a pretty good idea what their office looks like. If the car is immaculate, their office will probably be the same. If the car is cluttered, their office will be cluttered. This is not necessarily good or bad. It's just that there is a consistency of behavior you can predict will impact other areas of work.

Just by speaking to someone for five minutes gives you an idea of how they talk to others. *Are they patient? Do they make eye contact? Are they articulate?* If you're having lunch with someone, you can watch how they interact with the waitstaff and get a pretty good understanding of how they interact with their team.

This principle gives us the ability to take mental snapshots throughout the day, providing powerful insights into the people around us. Learning how each team member operates can open a door to helping our entire teams, including ourselves, operate at a higher level. It also offers insight into yourself.

You can watch yourself do one thing, and with that awareness, ask if that behavior happens in other areas. What are you like at work? How are you handling information and responding to events? Do your patterns of behavior work for you, your team, your family, and your community? Or is there room for change? When you see yourself acting in a nonproductive way at work, ask yourself whether you do this at home and vice versa.

If I see the same person at the dry cleaner every week for a year, and I can't tell you their name, does this say something about me? Do I only care about people who are important to my goals? Do I care about people for themselves? At home, if my spouse gives me feedback and I dismiss it, it should lead me to ask the question: What do I do with feedback at work? If I show up to a meeting where I'm not in charge, and I sit back and disengage, what does that mean? Do I have a pattern of refusing to add value when I'm not in charge? Is that a good thing?

Who you are in one area of your life is who you are in all areas.

Who you are in one area of your life is who you are in all areas.

Compartmentalization Doesn't Work

When I give people feedback about their lack of patience, poor follow-through, or irritability, and they convey to me that they don't care, I often respond with a question: How does this character flaw show up with your kids? Upon asking this question, many times their faces go pale. When

I confront someone who is micromanaging at work, I ask them: How does your spouse feel about the fact that you behave like this at home? This question puts bad behavior into perspective. When you commit an unproductive action at work, you will do so in other places as well—places where you care deeply about the people involved.

–Joe

Compartmentalizing yourself doesn't work. As the hero of the 1984 cult classic movie *The Adventures of Buckaroo Banzai Across the 8th Dimension* said, "No matter where you go, there you are." In medicine, the people who understand this the best are psychiatrists and psychologists. Part of their training is to examine their own pasts and their own feelings about their patients. This allows them to access unconscious elements of themselves that can then be used to make their diagnoses and treatments more intelligent. If you don't access and acknowledge those unconscious elements, they seep out when you don't want them to, and you can end up behaving poorly.

–Mike

Moving Beyond the Natural

Step 1: Ask yourself some of the questions in this chapter.

Step 2: Answer the question "What is one way your negative behavior at work might be impacting your behavior at home?"

Step 3: Think of one positive trait you have at home and plan to implement it at your place of work.

Notes

Maxim 5

THE LAST PERSON TO GET YOUR PERSONAL FEEDBACK IS YOU

We often think of personal feedback as a closed-door conversation between a boss and employee with the leader quietly telling their team member about the ways they can improve.

But the dirty secret is that feedback shared in these meetings is seldom information that is limited to the two individuals in the room. It's likely everyone who works with this person is already aware of the need for this conversation. Personal feedback is generally knowledge everyone knows.

If you are a leader, people are talking about you. There's always a conversation going on that you can't hear. Inside that conversation is valuable information. Your challenge is to become part of this discussion. That's what feedback is all about. It's an invitation to participate in the dialogue going on around you.

Leaders, like everyone else, tend to hate feedback. They would rather not know what others think of them. But if it's your goal to elevate your leadership, this is the wrong attitude to have. You must want to know what others think and what others say because you need to know what works and what doesn't. You must know what people like, what they need, and what they want to try.

People in charge of organizations are constantly frustrated that direct reports fail to share with them important details. But often, this says more about the leader than it does the employee. It's a sign the leader cannot handle bad news and has the tendency to "shoot the messenger."

To guard against this, make it a habit to thank people for bad news. Buy them a present when they alert you to a looming problem! If they point out something you did wrong, thank them. It's rare to find someone who will trust you enough to share feedback you need to hear.

Remember that when you as a leader make decisions, you impact people in tremendous ways. Your decisions will influence the organization's success far into the future because the people around you depend on that organization for their livelihood.

How Do You Request Feedback?

Feedback is best received when you start with a single question. Here are a few options:

- What's the one thing I can do to be more helpful to you?
- Is there something you're not sure I know that's important for me to know?

- If I were to hire you as my coach, what's the first piece of advice you would share?
- If you were to advise me on how to be more effective in this organization, what's the first thing you would tell me to do?
- What is something I do that tends to frustrate people or let them down?

When you get your answer, thank the sharer verbally, and use your body language to thank them. Take the extra step and follow up with an email the next day to thank them again. And then a week later, tell them what you're doing based on the comments they gave you. Follow this up with a statement like this: "If you ever have an idea on how to help me, I'd love it if you would share it with me."

This little formula is powerful. Through your actions, you have demonstrated you have listened, you will act on what they said, and they will not suffer any consequences. Now they believe you.

Always remember, when we as leaders are invited to listen to the conversation around us, the way we respond dictates whether we are edged out of future talks or kept in the conversation.

When we as leaders are invited to listen to the conversation around us, the way we respond dictates whether we are edged out of future talks or kept in the conversation.

How to Evaluate Feedback

Receiving feedback is emotional. Generally, positive feedback nourishes and renews us. Think about your life. Picture how great you felt when your boss said something like, "I've been noticing the care with which you greet everyone who comes into the store. I can't tell you what a difference you make to so many. In fact, let me show you these great comments that have come in since you've started working here."

Then there is feedback that is upsetting and deflating: "I cannot believe how careless and thoughtless you are," and "Do you have any idea the cost of the mistake you've just made?" and "We did not hire you to make mistakes. Next time, you're fired!"

Given the degree of emotion involved, it's important to think clearly about feedback before acting. Sometimes, feedback can be contradictory. You might hear, "Sally, you are a great communicator," and then, "You don't know how to talk to people." What do you do with that?

In these moments, remember that feedback is more about the *giver* than the *receiver*. People will tell you what they like or what they don't like about you and the workplace. And everyone has a different opinion. Your goal is to gather all your feedback and look for patterns.

Think twice before acting on a single statement from a single individual—especially when you cannot connect it to anything else you have heard. That individual may have a bias or a hidden agenda. Of course, they may also be the only person with the courage to tell you the truth. This is why evaluation is important.

Feedback Helps You Overcome Blind Spots

When you look forward, you cannot see what's behind you. When you focus on a single task, it's hard to see everything that's happening around you. As we grow up, we learn to focus on certain things and not on others. Sometimes, those seemingly insignificant details we've learned to ignore turn out to be important. These are our blind spots.

Blind spots are not always obvious, so look for patterns in your behavior that get you in trouble. Look for details in feedback that are painful—the ones you don't want to think about. Ask your friends and your family for their perspective.

Remember, your personal shortcomings are public knowledge to those who know you best. Make sure that you are not the one left in the dark.

Why Listening to Feedback Is Critical

Several years back I was working with an individual in one of the nation's largest banks. This leader had received feedback in the form of a 360 report and had dismissed it all as ridiculous. He had risen high within the bank, which in his mind gave him permission to discount anything he didn't want to hear. One day, after making no progress, I attempted to drive home the importance of this feedback. His wife happened to call during our conversation, and as he stepped out to hear what she had to say, I made one request: "Before you hang up, read a few of the feedback statements to your wife."

A few minutes later, a very sheepish executive reopened the door and invited me back into his office. The response from his wife was that the feedback was more on point than he thought. In fact, it was the same message she had tried to share with him for years. As he shared this interaction with me, he ended with these words: "Maybe it is time for me to start listening."

–Joe

My daughter's hobby is Olympic weightlifting. She doesn't compete at a professional level, but she just enjoys the sport. I have videos of her going through the complex motions of walking up to the barbell, placing her hands and feet in the exact right place, exploding upward with the weight, and bringing it over her head. When she was just starting, if you had put her in a room by herself with that barbell and some weights for a year, she would be far from where she is today. The reason she has grown at such a fast pace is the feedback she has received. All along her coach has been saying, "Your feet are too far apart," and "You're too slow on the second pull," and "That's all you should do for today." Feedback is what makes us excellent.

–Mike

Moving Beyond the Natural

Step 1: Ask your spouse, or someone close to you, this question: *How do I respond to feedback?*

Step 2: Approach one of your direct reports or supervisors you trust and request feedback by asking them this question: *Is there something you're not sure I know that's important for me to know?*

Step 3: Write down two to three blind spots you have overcome in the past three years. Now, ask yourself and seek help from others about other potential blind spots in your life today.

Notes

Maxim 6

DON'T ENJOY BEING RIGHT

Everyone loves to be right. It helps us gain status and power. It eliminates uncertainty, and it means we don't have to think about complexities or subtleties. If we believe we are right, it helps us not feel the fear of being wrong.

The need to be right may be an artifact of our school systems, which reward the *right answer* rather than encouraging problem-solving, questioning assumptions, or critical thinking. Nearly everyone has spent years learning that being right is being good and being wrong is being a failure.

Unfortunately, this need to be right only expands our blind spots. When we become attached to a certain viewpoint, it's tempting to ignore evidence and alternate perspectives. Everyone has this problem. We get locked into ideas we can't defend. This is something that often happens with political discussions, where belief in our own rightness gets in the way of our ability to see other perspectives, absorb new information, and understand complexity.

Clinging to rightness, and closing the mind to subtleties, hurts. It makes us abrasive, because no one really likes a person who can't admit they are wrong. It also blinds us to the faults in ourselves that feed this attachment to being right.

Taken to extremes, the need to be right leads to people quitting jobs or being fired unnecessarily. It leads to broken relationships, anger, and frustration both at home and at work.

If you insist on being right about something, you are dismissing the wisdom and thinking of everyone around you and substituting your own—which is unlikely to be superior.

Too often, a defiant need to be right emerges around issues that are not important. When the rightness becomes more important than anything else, relationships and organizations suffer and break down.

"Who is right?" is never the question that's really at hand. The real questions are "What works? What is effective? What is helpful to our mission?" If you insist on being right about something, you are dismissing the wisdom and thinking of everyone around you and substituting your own—which is unlikely to be superior. The organization's success, the family's health, and your own inner peace are all more important than being right.

The Need-to-Be-Right Problem

In real life, there are usually at least ten right answers to every question. Unfortunately, we were not educated to appreciate this. In school we were taught there was only one right answer.

Leaders who continue to believe there is only ever a single answer may survive for a time. But they do not inspire or bring out the best in their teams. They control and manage too tightly.

If there are ten right answers, this means other people are important. Their ideas, insights, and knowledge are needed. *Do you really have to prove you're smarter than everyone else on your team?* That's not the best way to get a team to work together. *Are you willing to step back and let others shine?*

In case you are reticent to do this, remember that others have done the same for you in the past.

View Yourself as the Least Intelligent Person in the Room

It's human nature to try and figure out where you are in the hierarchy. Depending on the culture of your group—your work team, company, family, sports team, and so forth—status may be conveyed based on intelligence, talent, education, charisma, or other qualities.

If you think you are always right and smarter than someone else, you are less likely to listen to them. This will result in missing important information and communicates that they are not valued. Whatever the nature of the hierarchy you're in, put yourself at the bottom. Be a student. See yourself as the least intelligent person in the room. It might be true, and it might not. Don't lose information because of your arrogance.

There is no one in the world who doesn't have something they can do way better than you.

Why Being the Least Intelligent Person in the Room Can Be a Positive

I graduated from a US medical school, but my residency was mostly with "international medical graduates." These were doctors trained mostly in India and Pakistan. They were top graduates of their medical schools, and some of them had been attending physicians for years before coming to the United States and starting over as interns. It was not hard to feel like the least intelligent person in the room. I had a thought during my first week: "Some of these folks know more medicine right now than I will ever know." It was humiliating, but it drove me to be better. I reexamined my study habits, my patterns of thinking, and my way of working. And in the end, I'm thankful I spent so much time with so many excellent people.

–Mike

Jim was a highly talented and intelligent executive. He had risen to the top of his profession and had a great track record of success. One-on-one he was a kind, caring, and pleasant person to have a conversation with. The issue with Jim came up when anyone questioned anything in his department or under his realm of control. When this happened, Jim not only would become defensive, but he would do something I had not previously seen anyone do. He would bring in several pages of documentation in order to prove he was right! This happened each and every time someone would question or challenge anything he did.

Jim was "right" a lot, but in the end, no one enjoyed working with him. After several years of trying to find ways to collaborate, the team finally had enough and expelled him from the organization. Being right wasn't enough. You see, you can be right and at the same time be the most ineffective leader on the team. Not once has anyone brought me into an organization to help determine who was right and who was wrong. The goal of leadership is to find a way to make it work. Being right and making everyone else wrong in the process is simply immature and foolish.

–Joe

Moving Beyond the Natural

Step 1: Do you enjoy being right in a conversation? If so, write out a few steps you can take to reshape this behavior and better listen to others?

Step 2: What is one way you can point out the "rightness" of someone on your team? How can you highlight their decision-making over your own? Now, make it a point to acknowledge them in front of others tomorrow.

Step 3: Ask yourself, *What is the one area in life where being right is hurting my relationships?* Now, resolve to change. Instead of proving your rightness, be willing to admit when you are wrong.

Notes

Maxim 7

PEOPLE AT WORK CANNOT HEAL YOU

Relationships have a way of repeating themselves. We're all familiar with this reality. We make the same mistakes interpersonally again and again. We date the same type of people, and our current relationships mirror our past relationships.

In the workplace, repetition like this can cause problems. It can lead us to assume someone at work will behave like someone in another area of our lives. We might try to protect ourselves from such anticipated behavior or take revenge on the person at work for how we were treated by someone in the past.

Employees can see the boss as their "mom" or "dad." After all, home is the place where we have our first formative experiences with someone else being in charge. If a person grew up in a home where respect and healthy communication were not present, or where violent conflict and volatility were the norm, they will have trouble fitting into a healthy workplace culture.

There's also the risk that for a certain kind of person, work will become a place they expect to be healed. Deep in their hearts, something is saying, *perhaps this is the place where I will finally find peace, where I will finally be accepted.* But it's not the job of the workplace to make someone healthy. Yes, it's the responsibility of the workplace not to injure you, but it probably shouldn't be the place where your heart and soul find healing and lasting peace.

How You Move Forward

The first step past these dangers is to acknowledge your boss isn't your parent. This is a different kind of relationship, with different expectations of you and different forms of behavior that are appropriate. It may be necessary, when strong feelings arise in you around your boss, to step back and meditate on this point. By doing this, you are effectively creating an emotional boundary, separating your innate emotions from your relationship with your boss.

We can change and adapt to new relationships outside the habits and patterns of the past but only through reflection, self-awareness, and emotional intelligence. Emotions follow thoughts, and thoughts follow emotions. Use your thinking to influence how you feel during interactions with your boss.

If you're the boss in this dynamic, the best thing you can do is show trust. If you don't, and you wait for the employee to prove themselves trustworthy, this may reactivate an emotional wound from the past. They may be brought back to the time where the message was that they were not good enough, not perfect enough. That sets the stage for the employee to start projecting onto their boss the parental mindset, where the workplace becomes an arena to try to please the parent.

By extending trust, we level the field. We emphasize emotionally that we are not the parent, that we value who they are and what they bring. We set the stage for an adult relationship.

Limit Your Time with People Who Drain You

Rather than offer healing, some people will suck the life out of you. But there are certain boundaries you can implement that will guard against this. As Baltasar Gracián said, "There is great caution needed in helping the drowning without danger to oneself."

When we spend time with others in the workplace, we develop relationships. If you take all the relationships in the organization together, they create a social network. That network has properties of its own, beyond what any individual might perceive. One property of a social network is that it acts as a transmitter of personal energy: alertness, emotional tone, and positivity or negativity.

Leaders tend not to appreciate how their energy affects their employees and how their employees' energy impacts them. When you are a leader in the line of sight of employees, it is critical to attend to your body language, voice, and choice of words. The team or organization watches your every gesture and mood change. What they see has an impact on them, on the organization, and on you.

Let's put energy into two categories. There is a negative, pessimistic, victimhood, helpless energy that drains and wears everybody down. On the other hand, there is a positive, creative, look-for-opportunity, can-do energy that builds people up. This begs the question: *Are you communicating possibility, creativity, and opportunity?* Or do you communicate defeat and a lack of options?

One place in which leaders receive energy is from the people around them. So ask yourself a few questions: *Who am I spending time with? What kind of energy do those people give off?* As you develop this list, you will likely discover there are people who drain you. While it's important not to judge them, it is equally important to understand that their energy affects your success as well as your mood.

Some might push back on this idea and say, "I can't fire someone for just being negative." Perhaps this is true, but it's also critical that we give these folks feedback about their impact on others. In the end, the workplace may be better without some on board. At the very least, minimize your time with such people—even if you feel sorry for them. You can recognize the effect someone has on you by paying attention to how you feel when they walk into your office or when their name appears on your phone.

Help Heal Yourself

While people at work can't heal you, it's possible for you to use your relationships at work to heal yourself on your own. For example, if you have a troubled relationship with your mother, you are likely to feel echoes of that relationship with any female boss. In routine situations, your emotions may become inappropriate and strong. Recognizing those emotions—and where they come from—gives you power over them and provides insight into your past and the shape of your emotional self.

–Mike

Roberto was a vice president in his fourth year at a large company when he began to notice he was not included in meetings where he expected to have a seat at the table. As I was coaching, I started to understand he was projecting negativity with his body language. The folks around were not digging in to figure out what was going on. Instead, they were finding it easier just to exclude him. As I spent time talking to him, he had a steady stream of complaints around not being valued. He took almost everything the CEO did as a personal attack.

As we dug into the situation, it was clear he had grown up in a home where his father never complimented, never thanked, and always criticized. There was a big hole left behind. He had been living his life trying to fill that hole by finding someone—anyone—in a leadership position who would acknowledge, value, appreciate. However, the hole was so big that even when appreciation came, it wasn't enough. This was ironic because he was highly valued and respected in his organization. He was looking for his workplace to heal the hole, which was something that would never happen. The saddest part was that instead of entering therapy, he quit and went in search for another job, likely hoping deep down that the new job would heal him.

–Joe

Moving Beyond the Natural

Step 1: Make a mental note of the relationships you have had in the past and take note of the relationships you have today. Are they the same? If so, come up with some ways to improve your pattern of relationships.

Step 2: What types of people drain you? After identifying this list, set safeguards in your availability to limit their access to your life.

Step 3: What types of people energize you? Now, make some concrete commitments that will see them play a larger role in your life.

Notes

Maxim 8

FEAR OF SUCCESS IS FEAR OF SEPARATION

Sometimes, people sabotage their own success. They don't meet a deadline, or they say something impulsive at the wrong moment. This tendency arises out of fear—the fear of being separated from something they care about.

The hard reality is that success separates you from others. It elevates you, allowing you to see and think differently. You gather new colleagues and are exposed to new information and ways of thinking. Your worldview changes, and this can create friction in your social sphere. As this transformation takes place, a successful person will hear statements like, "You think you're better than us?" Someone who gets a promotion will feel awkward around their old colleagues, who might start to talk behind their back. This is a separation, and that separation can be more frightening than failure.

It was Marianne Williamson who said, "Our deepest fear is not that we are inadequate. Our deepest fear is that we are powerful beyond measure." Everyone needs to feel connected to others. There are few things that are more important than happiness. When we feel those connections are at risk, we can shrink back.

In an odd way, failure unites us. We can complain together, feel equal, and separate ourselves from the rest of the world. We begin to ascribe certain characteristics to the rest of the world. *Their motives are bad. They are dishonest. They are greedy. They are out to get us.* But these feelings are disconnected from reality because the world is much more complicated than we picture. When you see people outside your group as bad, it's usually a massive oversimplification. It's also counterproductive to success.

The social system around you has a life of its own, and it probably wants to keep you right where you are. It will apply pressure on you to ensure you remain in your current place. This makes breaking away emotionally difficult.

Consider this common story: A couple with kids decides they want to better their lives. The mom goes to school to become a nurse. But the family sabotages their mom's success. They may not acknowledge it even to themselves, but their words and actions are aimed at making her feel guilty for not spending time with them. They complain because she can't care for them as she did before. They all know the best thing is for her to go to school, but the behavior around the system is stronger.

Success Can Feel Threatening

Success threatens your identity. Success in leadership means becoming your better self. That sometimes means separating you from that which is familiar and enjoyable. For example, you may be accustomed to late-night partying with your friends at a local bar. If you become an executive, you can't be seen in public drinking to the point of intoxication. *Are you ready to give up your Saturday nights?* Or you may be known in your social circle for your clever and quirky fashion sense, while accepting a leadership role might require you to tone down your look. *Is this adjustment something you are willing to handle?*

Your life experiences may have led you to feel an aversion to holding others accountable. You may prefer to think of yourself as everybody's friend, and you may need the deep affection of others around you. But you can't always have those things as a leader. As you are promoted, you will have to create accountability, and you will have to deal with your feelings and memories, one way or another.

In the end, you must decide whether the things you cling to are more important than success.

Success means becoming your better self. But your old self can be like a small child's teddy bear—comfortable, familiar, and reassuring. Going to school without the teddy bear can be terrifying. In the end, you must decide whether the things you cling to are more important than success.

You Cannot Please Everyone

A young man from a disadvantaged background worked the night shift at a hotel. He then moved on to become a flight attendant and planned to become a pilot. His life was moving forward, and he was heading toward success. But his friends didn't react too well. "They're telling me I'm a sellout," he told me one day. "It's hard to be around them anymore. They don't understand what I'm doing." This man was experiencing the separation associated with success. The fear of that separation holds people back as much as anything in life.

–Joe

We all have what psychologists call "transitional objects"— things that we hold on to to help us through difficult times. Think of a teddy bear. Any professional success or promotion threatens to separate us from those things. One of my "transitional objects" is having messy clothing and hair. I'm not sure where this attachment comes from (perhaps from my years of being a journalist), but it's counterproductive. It remains uncomfortable for me to attend carefully to my appearance. But I do it when I have to.

–Mike

Moving Beyond the Natural

Step 1: Make a list of your greatest "success fears."

Step 2: Have you sabotaged the success of others? If so, ask yourself what steps you can take to cheer them on.

Step 3: How has success changed you for the better? List three ways you are a better person today than you were before you were stretched.

Notes

Maxim 9

YOUR SHADOW SIDE IS DEATHLY DANGEROUS

If you've read this far, it's likely you are willing to learn and develop. This is important because this next section will be one of the hardest lessons we have to tackle in this book.

Each of us has a shadow side. This part of us is difficult to think about, hard to explore, and very tough to do anything about. Yet it is tremendously rewarding for leaders who do. For those who don't, it becomes a ceiling, a limit on what they can do and how far they can get.

Having uncontrolled behaviors will scare and alienate people around you. Not being aware of this part of your own emotions will impair your ability to manage others. If you don't deal with this, it will control you and make you think that whatever is happening is just fate.

The shadow side contains things we don't want to have or don't want to deal with. It encompasses blind spots we actively try to push away. It's full of fear and shame. It's critical, judgmental, angry, and childish. We all have seen the shadow side leaking out from ourselves or others. Frequently, this looks like righteous anger.

The shadow side's potential for uncontrolled, intense negativity is what makes it dangerous. When we don't have a relationship with the shadow side, it can emerge at exactly the most inappropriate time to sabotage the success of both us and our organization. It is large and formidable. You can think of it as being as smart as you are, only with its own agenda. It may be difficult for you to accept the idea that the shadow side exists.

Dealing with the Shadow Side

The shadow side is complicated, often having multiple layers that a book of this length cannot fully uncover.

That said, there is a path forward, and this may involve being mindful of your emotions, watching them come and go, and analyzing what they mean. You may find that prayer or meditation helps you gain insights into your shadow side. Two extremely powerful paths are psychodynamic psychotherapy and twelve-step programs. Both can bring profound self-knowledge.

The psychologist Carl Jung said it's important not only to investigate the shadow but to see where it came from. Understanding the source of the shadow helps us dissolve the darkness and bring in the light.

For example, anger is typically triggered by either something that violates a person's values or a prior hurt that has been unresolved. When anger arrives, if we have enough self-consciousness to identify it and hit pause, we can ask a few questions that defuse the situation and bring light to the shadow. *Is the anger coming from fear? If so, what is it about you that most scares you or that you find most threatening? Are your opinions being threatened? If so, what is the internal message you hold on to about being right or, more importantly, what it means to be wrong?*

The process is never complete. You will never find a single answer that will solve this problem. The shadow side will always be alive and changing. You will always be negotiating with it. Being a leader means you are constantly looking and watching. And in this case, you are looking within.

As soon as you develop a fixed model of your shadow side, a picture in your mind, and say, "This is it!" things start to decay. That fixed perception becomes an illusion that keeps you from looking at the real shadow side, which is constantly changing. There is always more and a fresh place for it to hide. That's why this path takes tremendous courage.

Don't Let Your Shadow Side Stop You from Developing

Life has two stages. The first one, which author Richard Rohr calls the "ego" stage, is when we step out of our comfort zone and expand our lives. We venture into the unknown. We test our limits and take our thoughts of who we are and find out who we might become.

At this time, it's important not to settle and to try, even when we are failing. It's that subconscious nudging that says, "apply for that next position." The important thing is to act. This is how we become our better selves.

Unfortunately, our shadow side always seeks to hold us back. It can make us afraid and give us a feeling of entitlement that will urge us to avoid uncomfortable challenges. Or it can blind us to opportunities.

The second stage of life is "soul." Now, we are developing meaning and purpose. In the soul period, we focus on people and ask questions around how we help, how we develop, and how we inspire so that we can move others not to settle.

After progressing to the "soul" stage, we may now look back at our "ego" stage and see our achievements as unimportant. But what is important is that we tried, fought through the fear, and expanded our limits.

These two stages of life are not necessarily limited to a certain age or stage. We go through each in turn in various areas of endeavor at different times. We can enter each stage at any age. In fact, a great leader will engage in both simultaneously.

The key is to recognize our shadow side and keep it under control.

Everyone Has Shadow Sides

I did my medical training in Buffalo, New York. It was a good education and has served me well. But it is true I was not trained at Harvard or UCLA. That has always made me insecure. I'm board certified in internal medicine, but still, I doubt myself constantly. As a result, I realized a few years ago that I can have a very critical view of other doctors' shortcomings. I think this attitude is rooted in insecurities in my shadow side.

–Mike

When I was thirty-two, I ran my first marathon. This happened only as I started looking at excuses I had made in the past. These were no longer valid. I now looked at the world as being achievable. As we expand and take on challenges, we then start to see the next opportunities. Being able to run the marathon made a lot of lies fall flat, such as believing

I wasn't disciplined or organized or didn't follow through. This allowed me to keep expanding after that. It allowed me to maximize this ego phase. This experience taught me an important lesson. We live under our own limitations, and if we don't expand them, we become their captive.

–Joe

Moving Beyond the Natural

Step 1: Make a mental note of your shadow side and list the ways it impacts you in a negative way.

Step 2: Note whether you are in the ego or soul stage of life.

Step 3: Ask yourself, *How can I limit my shadow side to improve my development?* Now, take one practical step to put this into action.

Notes

Maxim 10

ANXIETY AND FEAR ARE PART OF BEING HUMAN

Anxiety is a part of being alive. You cannot escape it unless you're medicated or dead. To pretend you are not anxious is to be disconnected and fake.

The trick is to turn anxiety into an ally. Anxiety tells you what is important and how much time you should spend on one thing or another. This is why you should embrace anxiety and listen. It is one of the qualities that makes a leader.

Sit with your anxiety and examine it. Let it tell you what it has to say. But be careful, because sometimes it lies to you. So take the opportunity to challenge the assumptions behind it. Let it point you toward something that needs to be done. Maybe you need to work on healing an issue from your past. Perhaps you have been ignoring someone or something important. It could be you need to spend more time with someone or something that makes you anxious, because there is something new to learn.

Leaders need time to think and reflect. When you do not set aside time for thinking, anxiety points to what you're missing. Pay attention to what triggers it and what eases it. Follow it to the problem. Don't be shocked by anxiety. To sit with it and watch where it leads are part of the inward journey of the leader.

Anxiety Leads to Fear

Anxiety may become fear—an emotional reaction to danger. Fear is anxiety's cousin and equally important. If I have no fear as a leader, then I don't understand where I am, I don't recognize the strategic plan, and I don't have real goals.

But how do I keep moving forward without fear? This is the million-dollar question. Even the most successful people are afraid. Leaders have a lot on the line, and they must make decisions that affect people's lives. These keep them up at night. The absence of a guaranteed outcome can be frightening. Leadership is moving forward into the unknown. It's being courageous. And as the great leader Franklin Delano Roosevelt said, "Courage is not the absence of fear, but rather the assessment that something else is more important than fear."

Fear leads the best leaders to question themselves. They pause, and they take their work seriously, because their decisions affect so much and so many. They're better when they have an awareness of who they are and when they are willing to let that awareness inform their thought processes. They see themselves, and all their baggage, as part of every situation.

Leaders can talk about things they do wrong and situations they fear. Paradoxically, this turns fear into confidence. Problems become smaller and more easily managed, rather than just in your head.

If fear has got a stranglehold on you, dispel the fear by seeking clarity. Bring in key team members and ask, "What am I missing? What don't I see? What don't I understand?" Asking in that way gives people permission to play devil's advocate. "How are things going?" is not enough. It's too vague. It doesn't create the safety that will allow people to speak.

The narcissist doesn't invite people in. The person who is insecure to begin with and becomes arrogant doesn't bring people in or welcome their perspectives. The healthy leader can listen and take feedback on board, rather than blindly staying the course.

Never Lead Out of Fear

There is a leadership style that arises out of fear. It is not uncommon. When we meet a person like this, we can't always define what it is that bothers us, but we can feel it. We feel dismissed, diminished, or devalued. The leader's statements feel disingenuous and contrived. We suspect there is another agenda. Conversation shuts down, and team members hold back.

This can happen to any of us. Our relationships deteriorate, and we stop listening. Others don't trust us because they feel we are trying to use them. We look arrogant. We have adopted a fear-filled, selfish mindset. "Power corrupts" because power like this is already a corrupted state.

Yet power and control have a time limit. People who have a choice will leave. They will stay as long as it takes to find a new situation where relationships are healthier and more equal. Those who cannot leave, perhaps because they need the benefits or have to live in a geographical area, will become miserable and disconnected with their work. Either way, the organization will suffer.

The antidote to withdrawing into fear is to be a servant leader. The servant leader does not command. Instead, they develop relationships. When you have good relationships, you can engage the hearts and minds of others and arrive at more intelligent and effective solutions to problems. You can invite others into the decision-making process. Positive relationships release energy that would otherwise be spent in individual self-defense. Your modeling of good relationships will propagate through the organization, and the organization will operate more effectively. The organization will be more likely to succeed. It will be more agile and coherent. It will more likely be focused on what matters.

Fear Must Be Overcome

One formative moment of my career occurred in the first few days of medical school. It was in a lecture hall by the Gross Anatomy Lab. There were several partially dissected cadavers on a table in the front of the room. It was crowded, and there were about eighty people between me and the door. The professor was talking about the muscles of the back, and I started to panic. I was standing in a crowded room with several dead bodies. I thought I was going to have to run out of the room. But then I said to myself, "You have to do this if you want to be a doctor." I reminded myself that my long-term goal was more important than my momentary reaction. This reframing caused me to calm down.

–Mike

A company president I coached tried for years to build a healthy team. He couldn't bring people together because a single individual was very negative. This person would not listen to any opinions other than their own. They would argue against almost any point that was brought up. As a result, executive team members found excuses not to attend meetings. Two silos developed: this one individual and his area, and everyone else. Gossip was everywhere, and the senior executive team was falling apart.

In my discussions with the president, I asked him why he didn't replace this one individual who was being so destructive. As I came to find out, he was afraid of making a decision and worried that if the business tanked afterward, he would be blamed. What he wasn't considering was how much his relationships with everyone else would suffer if he did not act. In fact, the longer this situation dragged out, the more he lost the respect of those he led.

As a result, when he tried to give feedback to other executives, they would always respond with something like, "Tell X to shape up first, then I'll listen to what you have to say." This company president was afraid. But by not dealing with his fear, by not confronting what most frightened him, he lost the relationships that were important to the organization's success. And by the time the individual who caused so much tension on the team was let go, it was too late for the president to recover. A year later he was dismissed.

–Joe

Moving Beyond the Natural

Step 1: Ask yourself, What is my greatest fear?

Step 2: Now, write down what it is about that fear that paralyzes you.

Step 3: Develop a game plan to confront your fear.

Notes

Maxim 11

YOUR RAT BRAIN WILL TRY TO SABOTAGE YOU

Think of the last time you saw someone so angry they could not think. Or picture someone who was so deeply in love they had serious blind spots about the object of their affection. These are extreme examples of the mind being overtaken by emotion.

We like to think of ourselves as rational, but sometimes rationality is only a thin layer covering our emotions and instincts—a layer that can rapidly malfunction if we are exposed to something that triggers our emotions. When this happens at work, it can cause damage—sometimes in a way that is not recoverable.

For this reason, it is essential for us to monitor ourselves, to watch for when our emotions and instincts become strong and attempt to take over. We might refer to this as the *rat brain takeover*. Rats are fine enough creatures, but they tend to operate on instinct, not reason. Our minds have the tendency to do the same.

This means it's important to notice when the rat brain is taking over. It might be hard to know when it's happening. Different people have different levels of emotional awareness in the moment. Some immediately know when they get angry, and some do not.

Rat Brain Causes Fear and Distrust

A leadership team from the manufacturing industry was gathered for an offsite retreat. They had collected data, assembled ideas, and teed up strategies for the group to consider. Then, early on in an introductory phase, someone used an expression that sounded funny to the rest of the group. The individual in charge didn't take it that way and grew more serious. The dynamic in the room began to change, and this leader became noticeably annoyed, uncomfortable, and irritated and started to nitpick and interject into the conversation.

As different team members tried to clarify his statements, it became obvious the group was not able to move forward. Suddenly, this individual in charge became red in the face, focusing his reaction on one person in the group, who up to that point hadn't even been talking. The leader became angry as the group watched his rat brain take over. Finally, a break was called as people huddled in small groups, trying to figure out what had just happened.

The meeting reconvened, and the leader tried to explain his behavior, to justify or rationalize what they had seen. But all of this was to no avail.

No one spoke the rest of the day, other than essential answers. The tension in the room never cleared. This leader never understood how irrational he had appeared. And in one moment, he lost credibility and respect in a way that would be hard to restore.

Guard Against the Takeover

If you're one of the people who lacks awareness, you might notice a physical signal that something has changed—your voice rises, your heart pounds, your face flushes, your back becomes tense, or your stomach feels upset. You may notice that you are sitting forward, tapping your fingers, or shaking. Your rat brain may show itself by making you feel self-righteous or justified.

Watch yourself when you know you are angry or upset. Be particularly attentive when you feel you are being threatened by someone or something at work.

What do you do when the rat brain takes over? The best thing you can do is *exit the situation*. Create space. Let your head clear. Whatever triggered you is still present in that situation, and you don't want to go into a frenzy. So get away. Take a walk, grab a coffee, or find some important errand. The process of calming down may take twenty minutes to an hour. For some people it takes much longer.

If you can't exit the situation, *stop talking*. Because what you are thinking about saying is not rational. You can't think straight with rat brain. You may feel that things are tremendously clear and that your cognitive processes are just fine. But trust us, they are not. You are not at your best, and you will not be able to engage your foresight, wisdom, and prudence adequately.

Know what's happening, get away if you can, recover, and come back to the situation with all your faculties. Don't limit yourself when a short break can make you stronger.

Rat Brain Can Happen to Anyone

One day during a senior leadership meeting at my hospital, we were reviewing a serious safety event. I pointed out to the team that certain administrative decisions we had made a while back had contributed to the situation. To my frustration, the other senior leaders didn't accept this idea. I persisted. We discussed it for a while, and eventually I let it drop. However, I had apparently become angry during the meeting. My rat brain must have acted up because the CEO spoke to me about it later. And during this follow-up conversation, I became angry again. This time I knew what was happening, and I was smart enough to ask that the meeting be delayed until I cooled down. I excused myself from the conversation before I made another mistake.

–Mike

A hospital system on the West Coast asked me to work with its leaders as the system grew. Part of the process was a 360-degree feedback process with all the executives. So one day we sat down to go over the results. There was a woman in the group who was highly regarded and very competent. She had never received feedback like this. As I watched the group, I noticed she had a tear rolling down her cheek.

I wheeled my chair over to her and asked her what hurt. With a faraway look on her face, she said, "I can't believe they don't think I'm perfect."

I asked, "Do you believe the way you work is perfect?"

"No, but I at least thought they would."

Something inside this individual made her think that people are either right or wrong, that you are perfect or a failure. The only thing she was able to hear in that moment is that she was wrong and imperfect.

Anyone else, looking at that same document, would have seen someone highly respected, highly valued, deeply cared for by the team and the organization, with minor things to work on. But her rat brain was released, and any message other than failure fell flat. Her rat brain was triggering her reflex of "fight, flight, or freeze." In this case she froze.

Over the next few weeks, she decided to leave the organization and get a fresh start. To those around her, this decision was irrational and shocking. It left the team feeling guilty and confused, as if somehow they had caused this irrational reaction.

–Joe

Moving Beyond the Natural

Step 1: Take note of what triggers your rat brain.

Step 2: If your rat brain takes over, take the time to explain to your team what happened and apologize.

Step 3: Now, come up with a game plan for the next time you are in that situation.

Notes

Maxim 12

BECOME YOUR BETTER SELF

The qualities that make a good leader are the qualities that make a good person. The best way to succeed at work is to make yourself into the best person possible.

A tremendously moral person cannot be summarized in a few words. That's because it's hard to define what makes a person good. The list of qualities is endless. It would have to include hard work, a positive attitude, accountability, responsibility, friendliness, courage, caring, self-awareness, trustworthiness, dependability, curiosity, and a learning mindset. Most people would say those qualities are desirable in and of themselves. At work, your job is to develop those qualities. Your job is to become a better person.

The qualities that make a good leader are the qualities that make a good person.

At work, we can examine our issues by watching where we are triggered or irrational, and where we have not listened adequately. We can learn that when we get angry, we should walk away, get a drink of water, and calm down. We can learn that while it's natural to express anger, it's not necessarily productive, because an angry leader triggers fear in many people.

We can change. We can learn how to overcome the parts of our natural selves that do not work. No matter where we start, no matter what we have, we can move toward the goal of being better people. A thinker can learn to feel. An emotional person can learn careful reasoning. A self-centered person can learn to listen. A shy person can learn to speak confidently before a group.

The Need for Good Leaders

The world needs diverse leaders, but it doesn't need bad leaders. Never before has the global work environment been more open to diverse approaches and styles of leadership. This means there is room for you and your style. It does not mean you are absolved from self-improvement.

Work is a laboratory where you can experiment with who you want to be and practice being your best self. You can decide to try different approaches. You can decide every day, again and again, because each day you can start over. Keep yourself focused on who you want to become.

The world needs diverse leaders, but it doesn't need bad leaders.

Don't be surprised if working on your weak points at work spills over into improvements to your life at home. The things that give you problems at work also give you problems outside of work. You are one person, not two, and the way you do one thing is the way you do everything else. Your work personality and your home personality are connected. Your defects affect the people you care about. Whatever is taking away the joy of work is taking away the joy outside of work. Whatever is sabotaging your relationships at work is sabotaging your home relationships.

At work, it is your job as a leader to resolve these problems. You are paid to lead, and that means you are paid to become a better person. You are therefore being paid for an activity that will make your home life better.

If you do not care about being a good person, act like you do. At least pretend that you care about being good. While this is not the best-case scenario, just going through the motions alone will bring you to a better place where you will develop better qualities and become better at leading people.

When I started out in a physician leadership position, I behaved naturally. That meant I would get angry from time to time. But over the years, as I watched the effect that angry people had on their environments, I saw this was counterproductive. I spent many years examining my own anger and defusing it. Now that I have improved, I'm convinced my family life is better. I still see people cringe when I get into a certain mood, but I have improved.

–Mike

Years ago, I was coaching a senior executive. We were going over his feedback, some of which was quite negative, and he told me he wasn't willing to change. He said, "This is just who I am."

I was not sure how to respond, so I simply said, "Well, since this feedback is from your boss and the Board, 'who you are' is a guy who is about to be fired." That got his attention. What got his attention even more was that, on reflection, this feedback was similar to what his wife and grown children had also told him. He was hurting the people he cared about the most.

With that realization, a different tone emerged, a softness started to ease into the conversation, and he said, "Maybe we should work on helping me learn how to develop a new me."

–Joe

Moving Beyond the Natural

Step 1: Take note of some ways you have overcome challenges in the past and improved yourself. How did this happen? What was the breakthrough moment?

Step 2: Write down one area you would like to be better.

Step 3: List one way you might experiment with self-improvement at work, so that you can be a better person in all areas of your life.

Notes

Maxim 13

ENERGY HAS LIMITS; SO DO YOU

Energy is a fundamental resource in leadership. Among the long list of things continuously requiring our attention—people around us, time management, the board of directors, brand reputation, and multiple other concerns—energy is often overlooked. We can't exhaust our workforce and ourselves. When we are drained and tired, we don't think as well, we don't stay fully present in conversations, and we don't explore as many possibilities.

So pay attention to what builds you up and what brings you down. Each of us has different needs for exercise, diet, sleep, stress management, and human interaction. Managing these energy factors is an essential discipline.

Managing energy is a moral issue because our happiness depends on it. When people pour 100 percent of themselves into work, thus depleting their energy, they cannot meaningfully participate in home life and relationships—those things that are the most important parts of their lives.

Thus, you have a personal obligation to do the things that give you energy. To be best for other people is to first be best for yourself.

You have a personal obligation to do the things that give you energy.

Your energy is a moral issue because your organization's functionality depends on it. When people see you managing your own energy, they'll know it's OK for them to manage theirs. As a result, the organization will adapt and respond to the leader's habits around energy management.

Employees Follow What They See

Sometimes, people will not feel comfortable coming in later or leaving earlier than the leader. If the leader is working twelve to fourteen hours a day but telling team members to work shorter shifts, then the message is incongruent. Most people, when presented with mixed messages, have learned to be guided by another person's actions as opposed to their words.

On the other hand, when the workplace sees leaders taking care of themselves, taking breaks, leaving at a reasonable time, acknowledging their limits, and generally staying healthy, it gives them permission to manage their own energy in a similar manner.

The visible ways we show up as leaders, also known as the optics, are important. People read body language, eye contact, and physical energy. Positive energy gives confidence and propagates through the organization. A look of defeat pulls the energy of the organization down. People will create a story. They may wonder, "Is there bad news coming from above?" It's vital for leaders to demonstrate energy. That's what gives a leader particular permission to close the door and refresh and renew, or go for a walk or workout, and to manage their calendars to create blank space between meetings.

Know How to Be at Your Best

When your workplace is injuring people or harming relationships, you must raise your hand and say, "I am at my limit." It's insecurity that leads people to stretch themselves too far. It's the fear of not being important, not being seen as a hard worker, or not being valued. Those fears take over and lead us down a path of martyrdom.

There is a myth that our bosses want us to work until we are exhausted. But this is seldom the case. Instead, the truth is that other people tend to give us work, and so long as we say "yes," they will keep giving us more. But as soon as you say, "I can't do this," the response from most reasonable employers is "OK, let's figure it out," not "You're fired."

I (Mike) had a crash course in managing my energy when I worked the night shift in hospitals. While there are people who find it easy to stay up all night, there are others who find this impossible. Personally, I fall somewhere in the middle.

But here is the challenge: when you have an emergency at 3:30 a.m., you cannot afford even a slight impairment in your ability to think. It's critical to be at your best. And so, I was careful to watch myself, experiment, and discover certain techniques that worked for me in high-stress work situations. Here are a few I found especially helpful:

- **Hydration:** One cause of fogginess overnight is not getting adequate circulation to the brain. And one cause of reduced circulation is dehydration, which is easy to develop overnight. We sweat when we work and drink caffeine, which may act as a diuretic. Drinking large amounts of water seems to help.
- **Compression stockings on the legs:** These push blood back toward the body and keep the blood circulating. They also seem to prevent leg cramps.

- **Vitamin D:** Living in the dark, we must make sure we get enough of this vitamin, which is a steroid hormone made in the skin by sunlight. With no sun, you must take a pill. When I work night shifts, I aim for at least two thousand units a day.
- **Sleep in a room that is dark:** Any daylight coming in through the windows, or any artificial light, reduces the effectiveness of sleep.
- **Avoid carbohydrates overnight:** There is nothing that puts me to sleep faster than two pieces of pizza at 2:00 a.m. Instead, eat protein in small meals.
- **Sleep time is sacred:** Make sure your family or roommates understand that waking you up at 11:00 a.m. is like you waking them up at 3:00 a.m. (People have a tough time understanding this.)
- **Spend one day a week in total relaxation:** Let yourself sleep or stay awake whenever you want. Obviously, if you have children, this is a challenge, but there are steps you can take to manage it. During your workweek, you won't get enough sleep during the days, and you have to catch up sometime.
- **Exercise before the night shift:** Even walking around the block for fifteen minutes makes a difference.
- **Use caffeine judiciously:** Some caffeine is OK, especially during the difficult hours (3:00–5:00 a.m. for me). But too much will dehydrate you and cause you to crash after a few hours.

These action steps increased my energy levels and helped me operate at my best. Each person is different, and so it is important to know your body. Recognize those times when you need to push through the pain and other points when you need to pull back and regroup.

Everyone has their limit. It's up to you to know yours.

Healthy Boundaries Are Critical

I met a president of a manufacturing company that made rendering equipment—the stuff that takes the guts out of the chickens and reduces them into another product. The more we talked, the more I could see this man was completely burnt out. This led to a conversation about managing energy and becoming more effective.

I encouraged him to close the door three or four times during the day to get work done, so he wouldn't have to do it at home. He insisted that in his environment that was impossible, that people would barge in, that they would be offended, that manufacturing would be disrupted, and that there would be chaos. After going back and forth for months, he decided to give it a try.

After three weeks he called me up and said, "It's amazing. I close my door, I get my work done, people respect it, and things are running as smoothly as ever." What he had failed to see is that not only was he in constant crisis, but that his constant availability kept the whole plant in a state of crisis management. When he closed the door, the organization calmed down, and people started to solve their own problems. He would go home feeling OK and not allow his job to consume his life.

The only thing that changed was his understanding that his energy was his to manage. Not only did everyone else notice, but the energy in the plant changed as well. This fellow argued for a long time with me that he couldn't close his door. That speaks to the rut and the patterns we get into. We are so comfortable with the patterns we create that we believe breaking the pattern is impossible or will lead to negative effects. We constantly need to adapt our patterns as the situation changes.

To keep my energy up, I have to watch what I do during the day. If I am careful with what I eat, limit my alcohol intake, exercise, and if at the end of the day I listen to music and go to bed early, I wake up feeling good. Every one of those things is in my full control. If I came to your workplace, you would notice that two or three times during the day I'd be going for a walk, either outside or inside—often for no more than ten minutes. I know I can only sit and think and talk for so long. Activity builds energy.

–Joe

As a physician, I view it as my moral responsibility to be high energy and clear minded to the greatest extent possible during every moment I am caring for patients. This requires attention and self-control. It has helped me grow up.

–Mike

Moving Beyond the Natural

Step 1: Make a list of those things that drain you.

Step 2: Now, make a list of those things that energize you.

Step 3: Establish a game plan that will increase your energy at those critical moments of your day.

Notes

Maxim 14

PEOPLE PLEASERS TEND TO PLEASE THE WRONG PEOPLE

When you are focused on making people happy, your attention is naturally drawn toward the 2 to 3 percent of people who are the least happy. These are the folks who habitually disagree, criticize, and complain. But these are also *exactly the wrong people* who should take up most of your time. You can't win them over. They just want to be miserable. So don't put energy into them.

Instead, put your energy into people who are respectful, ask good questions, and want to be challenged. They might debate a point with you and then say, "OK, I got it." They will not persist with a negative attitude. These are the people who are achieving goals and helping others.

It can also be a mistake to try to please your direct reports. You may think if you are nice to them and not pushing them that you are making them happy. But if you're too permissive, if you allow them to deviate from their tasks or the organization's goals, you won't excel, you won't get promoted, and you would not be preparing your team for promotion. Successful people like to be held accountable with an appropriate amount of pressure.

Who Do You Need to Please?

The first person you need to please is your boss. It's important for your boss to be happy with what you're doing. This means being aligned with their expectations and delivering on those expectations. Sometimes you need to disagree and push back, or say, "This isn't possible right now."

Most of all, pleasing your boss means being trusted to do what you say you will do, when you say you will do it. It means you speak up early when problems arise. You don't sugarcoat or hide those problems, you respect the person's position (regardless of whether you respect the person), and you watch your tone when communicating. It means you work hard to build trust and consistency in your relationship.

Next, you need to please your peers. Peers rely on you and your behavior to help keep the company's culture and standards consistent and enforced. Peers count on you to do your portion of the work and to obtain the necessary results from your team. Peers rely on you to tell them what you see and what you need. They rely on you to be honest and point out pitfalls rather than staying quiet and watching them fail. Peers rely on you to lend a hand when asked and to ask for help when you have a need.

> **Pleasing your boss means being trusted to do what you say you will do, when you say you will do it.**

Finally, you need to please your top performers: those on your team who are working hard and delivering the results that allow you to succeed. You please them by in turn not ignoring the underperformers but coaching them so that they either improve or move out. You please your best performers by doing the following:

- Giving them projects so that they can learn and develop into the next role
- Offering your time, so they have clarity and are aligned with you and confident about the work they are engaged in
- Praising their work and character in public to those above and delivering any negative feedback in private

The Problem of Being a People Pleaser

When I (Joe) was growing up, I inappropriately learned from my grandmother how to tell people what they wanted to hear. As a result, I started to make statements that were kind and acceptable but not true. This is classic people-pleasing. Someone would ask a question and, to not hurt their feelings or make them uncomfortable, I would tell them an answer that smoothed over the situation—at least for the moment.

There were two major flaws with my pattern of pleasing. First, I didn't realize I was protecting myself instead of others. I was the one who was uncomfortable with the truth and needed to learn how to be clear and direct. I was the one worried about their reaction and not allowing them to own their own reaction.

Second, I learned that protecting myself, or protecting others from the truth, is never, ultimately, pleasing or appropriate. A true friend will tell you what you need to hear. A supervisor tells an employee where they need to improve, and a peer lets a peer know when they are headed in a direction that leads to a cliff.

Tone and approach always matter, but the truth—as you see and understand it—is the truth, and facts are facts. By protecting someone, I could lead them into failure or a deeper mess. By addressing reality, the other person can respond and correct whatever is getting in the way.

When we step up and tell someone what others around them know but are not sharing, we are showing true care and kindness. When we stand by and watch someone flounder or fail without offering help, we withhold care and concern.

Today, I am pleased when I often hear the feedback that I tend to be clear and direct without sugarcoating while at the same time expressing care. For me, this has become my more mature understanding of what truly pleases people.

You Cannot Please Everyone

I practiced for many years in a rural hospital. One disadvantage to that environment is that some patients, and some of their family members, will assume you are incompetent. After all, why else would you be practicing in a remote location? When I was a younger doctor, I would try to engender confidence in such people by going through my training and experience and my faculty positions in the nearby city. But in the end, these efforts seldom worked. In my later years in the hospital, I would make a brief statement about myself and my qualifications, and then get back to work. If the patient and family truly did not trust me, despite my credentials, then I would often try to have the patient transferred to a city hospital.

–Mike

A highly intelligent young woman was being promoted to a management position. When asked how she felt, she said, "excited but scared." She was afraid her reports would become upset when corrected. After some discussion about the nature of the job and the importance of the role, she came to understand that people being upset was something she would have to accept and manage. After all, it's not practical for a leader to move a group of people forward without encountering resistance from time to time.

–Joe

Moving Beyond the Natural

Step 1: What does pleasing your boss look like? List two to three ways you can make them happy.

Step 2: Are there ways you are an inappropriate people pleaser? Do you tell people what they *want* to hear, not what they *need* to hear? If so, write down a few ways you will work to counteract this behavior.

Step 3: What does people-pleasing mean to you? Do you value it too highly? If so, work with someone close to you to set adequate expectations. Seek to perform your job well, without falling into the trap of receiving your personal fulfillment through pleasing others.

Notes

Maxim 15

HARD DOESN'T MAKE IT WRONG

Choosing the role of leadership means taking on various tasks, many of which are quite difficult—like firing people. The danger for the leader is thinking that because something is hard, it is wrong. It is easy to recognize the instinct that turns us away from difficult situations. Feelings can run strong around such situations, and somehow the strength of emotion can trigger our moral sense. We start to believe the situation is requiring us to behave in an unethical way. This then makes it natural to avoid the situation.

Remember, leadership is about overcoming our natural instincts, and great leaders generally do not act on instinct. When you are in a hard situation, it is important to separate the interpersonal difficulty from any moral issues that may be present. Generally, this will clarify the situation and make it easier to proceed.

A few key questions include the following: Is it truly wrong to fire someone who is dragging down a whole team? Is it wrong to confront a coworker about inappropriate behavior that is hurting the organization's mission? While these are difficult questions to answer, they are actions that are sometimes necessary.

As a leader, you are paid to do what is hard. You are paid to embrace the things that are hard. What makes hard tasks hard is the very fact we care. If we care about people, firing them is, by definition, difficult. Our values are in conflict: we care both about the person and about the organization. We don't want to be the bad guy. But just because something *feels* wrong doesn't mean it *is* wrong.

Leadership is about overcoming our natural instincts, and great leaders generally do not act on instinct.

Right and wrong are not the same as comfortable and uncomfortable.

It's Natural to Focus on Feelings

Attending to our feelings, and acting on them, is natural. Yet feelings do not always lead us to the highest truth and best outcomes. Naming them is one way to reduce their power over our actions. If you find yourself overwhelmed with emotion, take a break until you can identify your feelings: "I feel frustrated," or "I feel betrayed," or "I feel rejected."

This is why self-awareness is important. Self-awareness allows us to name those feelings, which is a step toward overcoming our natural instincts and taking the right actions.

Our instincts tend to turn us away from hard things. Yet the fact that something is hard often means it is worth fighting for and that we need to make it the focus of our attention. Many people ignore the hard parts of their roles. Instead of dealing with them, they create workarounds. They tell themselves this team doesn't work well with that team, so the organization moves another team to bypass the dysfunction. Or because this person doesn't do a good job, they move them into another role or create a different structure.

Our minds move away from hard things toward what is comfortable. As a leader, you must avoid that instinct. To find the things that are hard that you're ignoring, ask yourself questions like, "Who is the person I really need to be having a conversation with, and what does that conversation sound like?" or "What problems have I been avoiding that I can't avoid any longer?"

These questions can bring up items your mind has been putting away. They can help you focus on things you are avoiding because they feel wrong, even if they are not.

Sometimes Hard Is Good

Brian moved from CFO to CEO of a small company that had been bought for $10 million and now had a value of $5 million or $6 million. It was unclear if the company should be broken up, sold, or salvaged, and so Brian invited me to a leadership team meeting to work out a strategy.

To every possible solution, the team would bring up further problems and concerns. At one point I asked Brian to step out of the room, got the team together, and said, "Look, folks, this is your chance to turn this around and lead." We spent the next hour with the team unable to come up with one positive step to turn the situation around. Brian came in an hour later, saw that they could not solve any problems, and realized he had an extremely difficult task as a new CEO. He had the wrong team.

Over the next eighteen months, he carefully went about replacing the team and bringing in new people who could think, solve, plan, and imagine what the company could become. What he did over those eighteen months was as hard as anything he had ever done. He cared about those people but couldn't move forward with that team. Today, many years later, that company is a billion-dollar, international company. Being hard didn't make this job wrong. Often, the most meaningful transition times are the hardest times.

–Joe

Many times, I was the guy who had to talk to aging health-care providers about the fact that people were starting to worry about their performance. Most of the conversations were tremendously uncomfortable. However, it's clear they were necessary, for the benefit of the provider and for the community. It's always disheartening to me how few people are willing to initiate conversations like this.

–Mike

Moving Beyond the Natural

Step 1: Is there something you are doing right now that feels hard? Write it here.

Step 2: Now, evaluate if it is right or wrong.

Step 3: List some ways you can avoid focusing on your feelings when making important decisions.

Notes

Maxim 16

DOING THE RIGHT THING IS THE BURGER, NOT THE KETCHUP

Doing the right thing is important. It makes the work world better. It creates transparency and trust in organizations. It makes it easier for individuals to work for the common good without feeling like fools. In the words of Sophocles, it is preferable to "fail with honor than succeed by fraud."

People like to see the right thing done. Maybe you're super intelligent and work super hard. It's possible you believe this is enough, but in the end, other people will decide if you are successful. So you should do the right thing.

If life is a cheeseburger, doing the right thing is not the ketchup—it's the meat. There's a passage in Chinese literature from *I Ching* that says power and justice must be unified. They must be brought together at the same place and time for the world to function correctly. The description for hexagram 34 says: "When we understand this point—namely, that greatness (i.e., power) and justice must be indissolubly united—we understand the true meaning of all that happens in heaven and on earth."

What an audacious statement! Can everything in life be traced back to this concept? In fact, this is a thread that runs deeply through human life and history. Knowledge of justice without power is impotent. It is "a voice crying in the wilderness" with no one listening. It is knowledge without action. Conversely, the exercise of power without justice leads to corruption and ugliness. It hurts people, and people notice. History is filled with stories of corrupt and ugly leaders who are brought down by their own negligence of justice.

All human beings move toward what they think is good. Most of us have a measure of selfishness, and a measure of idealism. We work toward our own self-interests, for the good of our group, and the good of humanity. Pick one to take away, and you have one monstrosity or another.

There are people who love power, and there are people who love justice. The world works better when they work together.

Do It the Right Way

I could be fooling myself, but I like to think that power is not my primary goal in life. I would be happiest if everything was working as it should be, and everyone was getting what they needed. Obviously, that's not the case. As I have tried to work toward making medicine a better system, I have found myself moving into powerful roles. Also, moving into those powerful roles are people who just like power. It's tempting for me to see them as enemies. But in the end, we end up at the same place: I want justice, and they want power, and each one needs the other.

–Mike

In today's environment, the idea of the quick flip or the sudden rise and acquisition that leaves the founder and team wealthy has taken a negative toll on business. Too often people build for the short term, cutting corners and making decisions that they pray won't blow up on them before they sell. Sam was headed in this direction. He had a great concept, a brilliant mind, and the ability to gather great talent. However, the business was not being built for the long haul. The idea of building a company he would want his kids to work at one day was a foreign concept. But gradually, Sam began to work with the idea of building a company he might want to hold on to for forty years. As he did, he found his thinking and strategy started to shift. Culture, results, and building the right team started to matter over short-term success. Doing the right thing over the easy thing became core to his business.

I tell Sam's story because business is tough and scary at times. No one is ever sure if their business will work, if competition will show up out of the blue, or if they will fall on their face. But doing things the right way is key to giving yourself the best chance of creating not only something that might work and be successful but also something you might be proud of being connected to, if you or your children end up working there one day.

–Joe

Moving Beyond the Natural

Step 1: Think of the toughest situation you face today and ask yourself, *Why is doing the right thing so difficult?*

Step 2: Ask yourself, *What makes the combination of justice and power so great?*

Step 3: Write down one way you can combine justice and power for the greater good.

Notes

Maxim 17

BE THE PERSON OTHERS WANT TO HEAR

To get your ideas executed, you must get people to listen. True listening means being engaged emotionally and intellectually. You want your team to understand what you say and the reasons behind it but also *feel* the importance. If you can't get your team to listen like this, their work will be less united and focused.

To get your ideas executed, you must get people to listen.

To elicit true listening, you must demonstrate competency, compassion, and consistency.

Competency

When someone decides to join your team, they are making a bet. After deliberation, they have chosen you as their best chance for achieving their goals. Whether they are joining you to advance their long-term career plans or to have a stable job that allows them to care for their family, they are placing their confidence in you. They may have even uprooted their prior careers and families to join you. And when they accepted a position on your team, it was a bigger risk for them than for the organization.

Your team members are likely planning to stay with you for a long time (though, admittedly, these days that's about three to five years). But they need to be sure you are competent. They need to see you can achieve and that they are part of your plan.

The art of demonstrating competency is a big subject and varies by field. But there are certain nonnegotiables, as follows:

- You must admit when you are wrong.
- You must know the limits of your knowledge and skills and reach out to others when you are beyond your limits.
- You must attend to details when it is necessary—focusing on operations, monitoring what's happening on the front line, and deferring to your team members' expertise.

Compassion

It's natural to be self-absorbed. It's a survival skill when we are children, and many of us never grow beyond this phase. Leaders, though, need to do better.

They must get to know the dreams of the individuals on their teams. Leaders must know what drives them, understand their stresses, and know how to leverage their strengths and compensate for their shortcomings. Many organizational leaders fail in understanding the people around them, even though they are counting those same people for success.

Knowing your team takes time. More importantly, it requires genuine interest. As you learn their strengths, keep a lookout for opportunities for them to shine. Remember, we achieve our goals through the efforts of others, not just ourselves.

Be compassionate when others make mistakes. Remember the possibility that you may be partly to blame. After all, it was you who set and communicated expectations, you who did or did not react to past incidents, and you who—explicitly or implicitly—authorized the systems, methods, and resources they had to work with.

Consistency

As a leader, you must be consistent in energy, behavior, and demeanor. This helps your people feel secure, even in times of organizational change. When you pay attention to something, your people turn their attention to it as well. People read leaders' body language and facial expressions. If even one day you act like you don't care, people will remember.

This means you must control moodiness and send consistent messages around your belief in the team, the strategy, and its progress. You don't need to convey the exact same emotions every day. But you should be predictable and positive.

When leadership is inconsistent and unpredictable, chaos emerges. People begin to create stories about the leader, the organization, and their own performance. For example, "The business must be for sale," or "She is getting ready to take a job somewhere else," or "There are more layoffs coming." These stories are not productive.

If there is an external reason that will cause you to be inconsistent, communicate this with your team. If you must be absent to work on a project, explain the reasons for your temporary disengagement. As you go through a change as a leader, explain it over and over to your team until it becomes normal.

Following these three Cs of competency, compassion, and consistency will make you the person others want to hear.

Act Like You Care, Even When It's Hard

> In medicine, you do a better job if you have compassion for the patient in front of you. But you cannot do this for everyone. None of us are saints or the Dalai Lama, and some patients are just difficult to like. As a professional, you're responsible for remembering they deserve good care too. So even if someone is nasty and hard to deal with, you still need to act like you care—even if your emotions are having a hard time catching up with your beliefs. You pretend the individual is a member of your family, or someone else you care a lot about. You ask yourself, "What would I do for my closest relative?" then do that. You're not trying to fool the other person, but you're doing your best to get your mind into the appropriate space to provide good care. This is similar to a Tibetan Buddhist meditation where the practitioner focuses on this kind of love then tries to extend that same level of feeling out to a friend, then a stranger, then an enemy.
>
> *–Mike*

Jackie had been in a leadership role for two years. Watching her work with her team was impressive. She listened to understand and did so with incredible patience. She wanted to know how people thought, what they were thinking about, and why they thought the way they did. While listening she asked questions for clarity and understanding. When she needed to speak, she did so only after listening. What people learned in a short time was that she cared about people and what mattered to them. She cared about ideas and helping people improve their thinking and about learning as she helped others.

–Joe

Moving Beyond the Natural

Step 1: Write down what it means to be competent in your position.

Step 2: Write down what it means to show compassion to others in your workplace.

Step 3: Write down the key ways you will be consistent.

Notes

Maxim 18

LISTENING WELL REQUIRES SELF-AWARENESS

To be listened to or seen can be a transformative experience. To have someone else put their whole focus on you, your words, and the unspoken messages behind your words is one of the most powerful experiences you can have. When a leader listens at the highest level like this, team members feel validated, and the organization functions better.

Otto Scharmer stated, "If you are not a good listener, there is no way that you can develop real mastery in any discipline." Listening usually does not come naturally. A common complaint in the workplace is that supervisors don't listen and act defensive or preoccupied. Ironically, many supervisors complain that their direct reports never share anything with them.

So we'll state the obvious: *If you don't listen well, people won't tell you things.* Most leaders need to work on this.

Listening Requires Self-Awareness

Watch yourself while another person is speaking. You don't have to look them in the eye the whole time, but try to make eye contact and convey with your body and face that you are focused on them. If you are meeting over video, try to look straight into your camera. This communicates that you want to hear what they have to say.

Concentrate every part of your mind and heart for the few minutes you are listening. Ideally, bring everything that you are, everything you know, and everything you have experienced to bear on that single moment of listening. If your mind drifts off, bring it back. Don't think about what you are going to say next. When the other person is done talking, ask questions to make sure you understand. When you think you have the whole story, remember you probably don't. Try to convey curiosity and not blame as you inquire to find out what you are missing.

Listening Requires Practice

Listening is like a muscle that needs to be exercised. You can exercise your listening muscle by putting away distractions, paying attention to your body language, and making eye contact. You can work on the art of responding in short phrases to ensure clarity. You can look for the meaning behind the words and think about what is left unsaid. All this is important at work, but it's even more important at home, with the people you care about the most. This habit can make a difference in many areas of your life.

Listening builds trust. It gives your team confidence that when they have something to say, they will be heard. When this happens, they will see you not as defensive but as someone who is open to new ideas.

Listening is not subservience. You're not giving up your power or authority by listening. Listening is not agreeing. Listening is simply the respect and the courtesy of hearing what someone else has to say, so that dialogue can continue. The best answers come from compromise and collaboration, but these require listening first.

Listening Increases Your Competency

Listening makes your thinking better by incorporating the thinking of others. Throughout my medical career, I've seen that one of the biggest predictors of a doctor making bad decisions is not connecting with other doctors—in other words, not listening. If you try to think every problem out yourself without seeking input from colleagues, you neglect important sources of information that can help you achieve better outcomes.

–Mike

We learn to listen at a young age, but many never learn to do it well. Real listening is about focusing on what an individual is saying and how they are saying it. It requires that we calm our mind, focus our attention, and try to understand. Tim was a leader who thought he listened to his team, but in reality his team felt very unheard. Tim was not conscious that often in conversations—he would look at his phone, look away distracted, or jump into the conversation and offer a counterpoint before the individual had finished making their point. Listening requires self-awareness in that we need to pay attention to how we are showing up as well as what our eye contact and body language are communicating. When Tim received his feedback from the team, he was shocked to find that people felt he was in fact a very poor listener. Over the course of the next year, he had to learn to leave his phone facedown when people came in. He paid attention to his body language to make sure he was communicating to others that their time was important. He even practiced the skill of active listening to make sure his mind was not wandering. It was a tough change but one that was important to his overall leadership success.

–Joe

Moving Beyond the Natural

Step 1: Ask three people close to you if they would consider you to be a good listener.

Step 2: Are you a naturally self-aware person? If not, give others permission to speak truth into your life. Allow them to stop you when they feel you are not giving their words proper attention in a conversation.

Step 3: Practice the discipline of listening today. Give strong eye contact to those you interact with and seek to understand what they have to say.

Notes

Maxim 19

FEELINGS FOLLOW THOUGHTS

There is a popular idea that feelings are fixed and cannot change. Relationships, breakups, career choices, and life goals are undertaken based on this idea. Perhaps, in our supposedly hyperrational world, a glimpse of a feeling comes as such a surprise that it is treated as precious. Or perhaps this all is just a cognitive error embedded in our culture. In fact, thoughts and feelings interact all the time. Thoughts drive our feelings. Knowing this principle, and using it, is one thing that separates good leaders from great leaders.

Some individuals work with and control their thoughts, and therefore their feelings, so that their feelings work for their purposes. Others accept their thoughts and the consequences that come with them, including negative emotions. The former has much greater freedom. The latter are imprisoned inside their thoughts.

When we face a new situation, we have a first thought. There is an initial set of impressions and interpretations that comes up. We then have a choice as to whether we will embrace that first thought or not. We have the ability to keep it or discard it for one that works better. There is always a more positive way to think about something.

Think Well

In lieu of data, we make up stories. "We are too much accustomed to attribute to a single cause that which is the product of several, and the majority of our controversies come from that," said the Roman emperor, Marcus Aurelius.

There's something about the human mind that hates an absence of information. We have a drive to make a picture complete, to finish the story. We fill in between the lines. We interpolate between data points. Sometimes, the interpolated information is sufficiently accurate, and sometimes it's not.

This tendency is useful when we are trying to develop a coherent picture of a situation with incomplete data. First, bringing everything together into a complete model makes it possible to develop clarity and move forward. With a fractured map of the world, it's hard to make decisions. Also, this tendency is emotionally beneficial. When the situation is easy to summarize, it's less anxiety provoking, and a clear course of action focuses the mind and relieves the heart of worry.

However, as we make inferences with incomplete information, we forget our assumptions. We move on as if those inferences are solid facts. Our minds turn away from the uncertainty, and we even forget it is there. Uncertainty is relegated to the shadow side of our minds. In this way we embrace untruths and base our actions upon lies. This is bad for business, and it's bad for the relationships and structures of life outside of work.

The answer to all this is to keep questioning your own biases and watch for your own assumptions. This is exactly why you as a leader must have time to think, review, and contemplate.

Make no mistake, questioning biases and assumptions can be painful. Lots of times, we hang onto them because they are comfortable and give us some measure of peace. It's never pleasant to give up comfort, yet this is often what reality calls us to do. The deepest learning is sometimes unpleasant. Thinking is painful, and this is why it is hard to learn.

A story is never as accurate as reality. It's always just a model. Reality is endless, endlessly changing, and new. Stories only take us so far, and they tend to become less accurate and reliable with time.

Feelings Should Not Paralyze Us

Tim received an email from his supervisor on Friday, saying, "See me first thing Monday morning." The weekend was ruined because Tim assumed the worst. He couldn't afford to lose his job. He had a new house and a third child on the way. He couldn't sleep, barely ate, and was irritable with his family. It got so bad he actually started calling his network to find a new job. Finally, he walked into the meeting Monday morning exhausted, distraught, and angry at the world. To his surprise, the supervisor only wanted Tim to take over a new department that was in trouble. In the process, he received a raise! His thoughts and feelings could not have been more inaccurate.

–Joe

On the TV show *Restaurant: Impossible*, restaurateur Robert Irvine rapidly turns around failing eateries. During the COVID-19 pandemic, he went back to see how his former clients could be helped. In all cases, the owners thought the pandemic was negative and costly, and there was nothing they could do. Irvine came in and redesigned the menu and marketing, put up outside seating, and showed them that even in a global crisis, they could do catering, takeout, or outdoor seating. In the end, the only thing he did was change the way they thought. Those thoughts determined their emotional reality and their outcomes. He took them from "there's nothing you can do about this," to "there's a lot you can do about this." That led to a path of surviving the pandemic.

–Mike

Moving Beyond the Natural

Step 1: Ask yourself, What are some ways I can control my feelings today?

Step 2: Ask yourself, What are some ways I can question my own biases?

Step 3: Do feelings tend to paralyze you? If so, develop a strategy for the next time you feel overwhelmed.

Notes

Maxim 20

YOUR MENTAL MODELS MAKE YOU LAZY

It's a natural tendency to look for patterns, then weave those patterns into stories, hypotheses, or equations.

But let's think of all those stories, hypotheses, and equations as models—as pictures of reality rather than reality itself. When we make these models, we must leave something out, because, after all, reality is infinite and profoundly complex.

Jean-Martin Charcot stated, "Theory is great, but it doesn't prevent something from existing." Once we have models, it's natural to use them to interpret everything around us. When we were young, we had few models, and the world was full of wonder. But with more and more models, the world becomes more predictable, but it can lose some of its luster and become reassuring yet dull.

As this reassuring predictability encompasses our minds, we face a deadly trap. We can start to think we understand completely, or well enough. We stop looking for the new. We stop seeing things that don't fit into our patterns. We become lazy and fall into ruts.

One escape from this trap is through meditating on the idea that we really don't know much and that our models are limited. Plato tells us that Socrates's motto was "I know that I know nothing." It's useful to take this idea and use it as a hammer against our ideas and assumptions, to see if they are fragile or not. For example, "What do I believe I know about my competition, and do I really have any evidence for it?" or "I believe my product will be useful far into the future, but do I really know this?"

Develop Beginner's Mind

Another way to escape being blinded by our patterns is the Zen concept of "beginner's mind." This involves being open and eager when approaching any task, even a basic or menial one, to perceive what one has missed previously.

These approaches create insights that lead to a disruption in our perceptions of our environment. They will lead us to understand that just because a model works, there may be nine other fantastic models and nine other ways to do what we are doing.

Sometimes, circumstances have a painful way of showing us our models are inadequate. This kind of disruption can be scary because it forces us to give up our concepts in a less-than-controlled way. As children in school, we were taught the most important thing was to know the right answer. So it feels terrible when our models are proven wrong.

But real leaders must be comfortable with being uncomfortable. Unfortunately, many leaders are closed-minded and afraid of losing control, afraid to admit they don't have the answer. But there's nothing to be afraid of looking at other options. It's enriching and a bit like reading a book, even if you don't agree with it. It's not a waste of time, because it causes you to reflect.

It's rarely a waste of time to listen to someone.

Break Unhealthy Thought Patterns

In medicine, it's dangerous to get too comfortable with the diagnosis you have made. You can start to see everything that happens as a natural consequence of the diagnosis. Even unusual symptoms of illness can be attributed to your diagnosis, if you cling to it hard enough. A good physician knows there's always a chance something else is going on. A simple example is a patient with pneumonia. Frequently, they will require large amounts of IV fluids. This then causes some mild overload—congestive heart failure. But the patient's ongoing shortness of breath can be attributed just to the pneumonia, even when they start complaining about swollen legs.

–Mike

Years ago, I watched a series of videos produced by Dewitt Jones, formerly a photographer with *National Geographic*. The most striking line I remember is "getting the right photo frees you up to find the next better shots." Dewitt was making reference to the fact that there are countless good answers. Once he finds a shot that will work and the pressure is off, he then goes in search of even better shots (his work is amazing). It is important for leaders that we understand finding the answer isn't always the end of the searching. Finding the answer can take the pressure off in such a way that it frees our minds to consider and find even better solutions. Mental models can make us lazy if we stick with what we know and stop searching for those things we are yet to know but that could add great benefit to our organization or team. We know what we know, but the same is true that we don't know those things we don't know.

–Joe

Moving Beyond the Natural

Step 1: What is an example of a lazy mental model you have overcome in the past? Now, ask yourself how you can take the same approach with a new challenge you face.

Step 2: Ask yourself, How can I develop beginners mind?

Step 3: Is there a model in your life that is inaccurate? Write down some ways you can make a change.

Notes

Maxim 21

ALWAYS UPDATE THE STORIES YOU TELL

Every organization has stories that are fundamental to their culture, strategy, and design of daily work. These stories are based on limited data and are thus inherently incomplete. They must be regularly updated for the organization to function. In particular, stories about individuals must be updated to maximize each individual's ability to contribute to the organization's success.

"Stories" here refers to the models or paradigms that are used on a daily basis for an organization or an individual to understand the world. They may not actually be stories with a beginning, middle, and end. They may be sayings, ways of behavior, or shortcuts in thinking. They serve as touch points to make sure everyone is working together toward a shared goal that is rational and achievable in the current marketplace.

No story or model is good enough to last forever because reality is infinitely complex. Even at the moment a story is created, it cannot possibly account for every detail of the situation, never mind the change that inevitably occurs. A consequence of this incompleteness is that when we focus on a story and fail to update it, we start making mistakes over time. The story can start blinding us to new facts. It is as if the organization must navigate a landscape with an inaccurate map.

There is resistance to changing stories. First, it takes work to update a story, and we have enough work already. Second, we often use our story to justify our behavior. If we update the story, we must adjust the behavior, which also takes work. Third, there can be an emotional attachment to certain old memories of events. These have a way of remaining fresh in the mind, even if they are old, and those memories hold a grip on the story.

It's incumbent on us to update our team's stories continuously. This involves stepping out of the story, entering back to the reality underneath it, and learning something new. This must be done over and over. There is always new data coming in. And as people who want to see ourselves as thoughtful and intelligent, we must acknowledge we are operating on assumptions. It is then up to us to find a new story and bring it back to the group. Many times, this involves poking a hole in consensus reality, wading through potential changes, and having something of value to offer.

It's particularly dangerous not to update your stories about the people around you, because they are the core asset of your business. Updating these stories is best done through face-to-face interactions, which are at the core of the social world. When we speak with someone face-to-face, we receive a maximum amount of information about them, and it's easier to see them as a person. When we have minimal or no face-to-face interactions, our stories about them tend to become more static and stereotyped.

There just isn't enough time to have deep conversations with each of the one thousand people in a company. As a result, we must rest on brief concepts and shallow understandings of most of the people around us. It is imperative that we treat those concepts as provisional and acknowledge their incompleteness. There are no "simple" people.

We need to focus on continuously improving our understanding and knowledge of the people around us. As the late Peter Drucker instructed, "Knowledge has to be improved, challenged, and increased constantly, or it vanishes." For practical reasons, we need to focus this activity where it counts. For example, there may be an individual who we find annoying, but we are forced to work with them. Rather than begrudging this interaction, we should prioritize our time with this person, because there is something there for us to learn.

Why It's Important to Update through Listening

When I'm in a meeting, sometimes I imagine the meeting as a big blob of minds in the middle of a table. An assertive speaker may control how the blob is moving. Maybe that's appropriate. But it's possible the assertive speaker is getting caught up in their own thoughts. And maybe the quietly annoyed individual in the corner needs to ask a question or make a suggestion to make the blob smarter.

–Mike

Years ago, I was terribly unorganized. I flew by the seat of my pants and relied on memory to keep things straight.

That strategy worked fairly well until one day when everything came to a crashing halt. I found myself in Maine, dropping quarters into a phone booth, trying to figure out which hotel had a reservation in my name and trying to identify the location I was scheduled to meet the folks who were expecting me. The sun was setting, and I froze. At that moment I made a commitment to get myself organized.

I started to use a personal scheduling system. I started keeping things in files. And gradually, life became less chaotic. Fast-forward twenty years, and my wife, Theresa, and I were preparing to move our residence from one state to another. She was helping me pack my office when suddenly she looked at me and asked, "When did you get so organized?"

I was a bit startled and replied, "Twenty years ago." We had been together for a long time. During our early years, she knew me as a disorganized mess. But I had changed, while her previous story about me remained in place. It's important to update our stories as people and things around us continue to change and evolve.

–Joe

Moving Beyond the Natural

Step 1: Ask yourself, What is a story I need to update?

Step 2: Now, decide how you can do this in a way that changes the narrative moving forward.

Step 3: Develop a system that will help you update the stories you hear in the future.

Notes

Maxim 22

UNCERTAINTY IS NOT NECESSARILY A BAD THING

Nothing is certain. Competitors will surprise us with something new. Key staff members may fall ill. There may be weaknesses in the supply chain that only a catastrophe will bring to light. Someone we trust today might already be stealing from our organization. As we're writing this, the COVID-19 epidemic has dealt an enormous, unexpected blow to every business, and the effects will echo for years to come.

At the risk of stating the obvious, humans hate uncertainty. To cope with it, we fall into one of three patterns.

Pattern 1: We Turn Away

We turn our minds away from the unknown and pretend we really know what's going on, that we understand what's going to happen or what the truth really is. We tell ourselves a comforting story and cling to this narrative. Doing so is natural, and usually we are not aware of what we're doing.

Consider these two examples. Senior leadership has engaged a new consultant who is asking a lot of questions. Nervous staffers tell themselves, "This is just another consultant who will make a report that nobody reads." Or there's a rumor that a key supplier is considering an exclusive contract with the competition.

You might respond, "They'll never do that to us because of the volume of business we provide." But in all honesty, you don't know these statements are true. Instead, you say them in your mind because they make you feel better.

Another way to think about this tendency is "jumping to conclusions."

Pattern 2: We Fight Uncertainty

Sometimes, we frantically try to figure it all out, to make the uncertainty go away. For example, we don't know about the reliability of some equipment, so we read up on the specs and put it through extra testing. We don't know if our employees are wasting time, so we install monitoring software on their computers. We're not sure what the next disruptive technology will be, so we start to read every relevant website we can find. But none of those courses of action can predict the future with absolute certainty.

It's a great thing to have the courage to investigate the unknown. It can take a level of honesty and determination that are not common. Yet this approach has limits. We cannot investigate everything. Even when we find what looks like an answer, it might prove to be wrong, or only partly right. We're still at risk of telling ourselves stories that are not completely true.

Pattern 3: We Get to Know Uncertainty

This is the wise path. We don't ignore the uncertainty, and we don't fight it. We acknowledge it, sit with it, and get to know it. We learn what we can and accept what we can't. We watch it change. We see what we can do with it.

For some, this requires a shift in thought. And for this reason, we suggest that when there is an important question at hand, sit down with your team and ask them what they know and what they are curious about. If you label uncertain things as matters you're curious about, they become less threatening, and the environment will be more agile and adaptable.

If there are no answers to certain questions, the questions become the data. Say to yourself, "I don't know why this competitor is acting in this way." Don't say, "They must have found some cheaper inputs," because that thought might solidify into a "knowledge" that is not based on facts.

Our natural defenses want uncertainty to go away. It makes us uncomfortable. But thinking clearly sometimes means you must think while you're uncomfortable.

Our natural defenses want uncertainty to go away. It makes us uncomfortable. But thinking clearly sometimes means you must think while you're uncomfortable.

We learn and adapt as the data instructs. Data and plans aren't as important as the outcome and the process of learning. As Eisenhower said, "Plans are useless, but planning is indispensable."

Thinking about control helps us understand this. When leaders believe they can control the future, they are not able to adjust to what is real. There will be fear and defensiveness, and learning will stop. This always leads to failure.

Sometimes it may be appropriate to be highly controlling. The surgeon should control the operating room: the process, the instruments, the climate, and the music. The sergeant should control how her troops behave on duty. The difficulty becomes separating where it is appropriate from where it is not. To apply that same level of control to how their yard is cut, or how the children behave, is not appropriate. A leader learns to exert control when it's appropriate and back off when it is not.

Replace Judgment with Curiosity

Curiosity is the antidote to judgment. So long as we remain curious, we allow people to remain engaged. By asking questions rather than telling, we give people the opportunity to allow us into their thought processes in a productive way. They can help us understand, we can help them understand, and together we can take the discussion to a higher level.

As leaders, we need to recognize the danger of judging others. For most of us, the immediate reaction to being judged is to withdraw. We do this by emotionally shutting down in place or by physically getting up and leaving. When people feel judged, they often stop contributing their ideas. They may even decide to leave the organization. Both approaches carry a cost that quickly becomes unacceptable.

Judgment never feels good and is disrespectful. It's our shadow side leaking out. No one typically sees themselves as highly judgmental and critical. Yet judging others is part of our human nature.

Sometimes Our Judgment Calls Are Incorrect

You can see this in medicine, where, in areas of uncertainty, doctors will start stringing together hypotheses to make a coherent story. The story is useful for explaining things and as a basis of action. However, it may not be a durable explanation of reality, and it's never a complete one. After all, there are forty thousand new medical articles published every month. Stories that embody hypotheses must be continuously questioned and updated. That's what science is.

–Mike

Back in the early 2000s, I was working with a tech company that was approaching a major decision regarding their platform. One person on the team believed that the future would be the phone, while the majority felt that desktops would always be the most important medium. The desktop group won out in this decision, but obviously they were wrong in the long term. Within a short period of time, with all the rapid technology changes, the company missed their window and was no longer financially solid. Just because we believe something is true, it is not necessarily so.

–Joe

Moving Beyond the Natural

Step 1: Do some self-evaluation. How do you handle uncertainty?

Step 2: Take note of the three patterns shared in this chapter. Which one do you gravitate toward and why?

Step 3: Ask yourself, What is one way I can replace judgment with curiosity?

Notes

Maxim 23

THERE ARE TEN RIGHT ANSWERS TO EVERY PROBLEM

When we were young, we discovered there are right and wrong answers. We learned that the capital of France is Paris, that 2 + 2 = 4, and that the sky is blue. The world is one way, and it is not another. It is correct to think of gravity as a law but not to think of gravity as a cake flavor. Years and years of our lives are spent learning facts, then learning the correct way to think about these realities. We are taught that truth doesn't change, and the right answer is always the only answer.

But as *National Geographic* photographer Dewitt Jones once said, "I realized that one of the great lessons of photography was that there was more than one right answer. If your approach to photography is to find the one 'perfect' perspective on a subject, keep going."

When we enter a position of leadership, we routinely deal with questions that do not have a single, clear answer. What is the best strategy in response to my competitor's new price point? How do I maximize the creative operation of my team? Where should I build my headquarters? Every answer you choose to each of these questions will lead you to a new situation, with new possibilities and new outcomes. There is no single right answer.

Take this common question, "What should the dress code be for our organization?" Answers may vary from business to business, as follows:

1. Business
2. Business casual
3. Casual
4. Business with Friday casual
5. Business with Friday business casual
6. Business casual with casual the first week of every month
7. Casual with business with outside client interactions
8. Business with casual as a reward for supporting a charity
9. No dress codes
10. "Dress for your day"

In the average company, consider how many hours of meetings have been spent making one of those options the right one and some of them the wrong ones. And any decision that was made was dependent on one's assessment of what is right for culture at any specific time.

If we hold on to our childhood perspective and think there is only one right answer, bad things will happen.

We Stop Listening

If we think we have found an answer, sometimes we do not feel we have to accept that other people might have good answers as well. We close off our minds to other options. But this decision comes with a cost. When there is no uncertainty as to a course of action, we do not spend time thinking about alternatives.

When leaders make a habit of not listening, people stop thinking and just wait to be told what to do. There used to be an expression in manufacturing: "Check your mind at the door." That meant you were hired to do something, not hired to think about your job or anything else. This attitude is still around. It's there, lurking under the surface, springing above the waterline when you see a boss who believes they have all the right answers.

Even the manufacturing industry found it to be unsustainable. Harley-Davidson was an early adopter of a policy that allowed any employee at any time to stop the entire production line of motorcycles when a problem was spotted. Before this, Harleys were coming off the line and leaking oil onto the floor of the dealerships. The result was dealerships were failing. In hospitals, major infection control breaches can be identified by custodians, if they are empowered to speak up. We don't want people only to speak up when they agree with us. Right-versus-wrong thinking teaches people we don't value their thoughts.

Get Past "One Right Answer" Thinking

We may have trouble getting past "one right answer" thinking because of insecurity. We falsely believe that because most people think there is only one answer, if we don't have it, people will think we're incompetent. But the truth is that at a certain level, leaders face difficult problems with more than one answer, and it's actually bad for your image to insist on one answer. You may be seen as someone who always needs to be right and who can never admit to being wrong.

Instead, think to yourself, "This is a complex question with many different opportunities. Who can I invite into the conversation to ensure we examine as many sides as possible?" Remember that you have people around you who can help you process options and decide. It's a strength to be able to do this, not a weakness.

You will still feel insecure from time to time. If you don't accept that insecurity and accept there are many answers to a problem, and that a team thinks better than any individual, this could evolve into a blind spot and a character flaw. You don't want that. You want to be the best possible leader, and to be your best you must be able to think along with a team.

You can see the folly of our right-versus-wrong thinking, because when we set something aside as "wrong," it remains so until it becomes a necessity. Working from home is an example. It might have been seen as an opportunity for employees to abuse the employer, but during the COVID-19 epidemic it became essential for many jobs. Video visits with doctors are similar. Many people believed they were not as good as meeting in person, but in certain situations it became the best way to take care of medical problems. If we cling to right-versus-wrong thinking, we can be slow to explore options and different points of view.

The Value of Looking Beyond One Way of Thinking

A company purchased a huge new facility. They moved in the same week that COVID-19 virus cases were starting to rise. Then the economy crashed, and everyone was forced to work from home. People at the company liked working from home, and soon the conversation changed to "Why did we think we had to move?" Tremendous money would have been saved. People would have been happier. And it would have been more consistent with who they are: a support organization. During the decision-making process, people in the organization had advocated for moving some jobs to remote but were shut down and told "no." The leadership couldn't have predicted the pandemic, but they could have made decisions that reflected greater listening while giving the organization greater flexibility.

–Joe

Hospitals are tremendously complex businesses to run, and they exist on small margins. Trying to improve margins was a constant strategic problem in our senior leadership meetings. There was no single right answer. Each had their downsides, and leadership had to decide which were palatable and which could not be borne. Here were some common options discussed: Cut back merit raises. Work with the pharmacy to find savings opportunities with manufacturers. Cut nursing staffing on low-acuity floors.

Terminate low-value services that are infrequently used. Outsource a service to a vendor. Open a new outpatient line of business that is a profit center, like a vein center. Screen for diseases in the community, hoping to bring surgical volume in. Billboards. Develop public trust, so people choose our emergency department when they are sick. Incentivize providers to see more patients.

–Mike

Moving Beyond the Natural

Step 1: Reflect on your upbringing. Were you taught there was only one way to think?

Step 2: Now, ask yourself how this way of thinking might hinder your ability to see better options on the table.

Step 3: If you are in the midst of a critical decision, take the step to look at alternative suggestions this week. See if there might be another "right" way to do it that is even better than the current option you see.

Notes

Maxim 24

YOU MUST CONTINUALLY LEARN AND ADJUST

We get our jobs based on what we know, what we've done, and how smart we are. These qualities are the cost of even being considered for a job. They do not set one apart.

Consider a major textile company that thought their technology was special. They never sold their old equipment for fear of competition acquiring their competitive advantage. One day they realized other companies had created equal or better machinery than what they were trying to protect. And suddenly they felt rather foolish for having large barns filled with worthless old equipment they once believed to be valuable. Knowledge is like this.

Today, what sets individuals and teams apart is their ability to come together and solve problems, fix mistakes, and identify key strategies for moving forward. They cannot hang on to knowledge as if it were some secret power. Instead, individuals and teams must share it freely within the workplace.

All of us together are smarter than any one of us individually. What we know is no longer what is most important, but rather how quickly we can learn what it is we need to know today.

Are you making the same mistakes over and over? Is your team coming together and asking, "What have we missed?" Are you making time for the conversation that starts out, "If we were brand new today, how would we best approach this business?" When you hit obstacles, do you fall back on the old information because it used to be enough, or do you seek to understand what has changed?

Being smart is important. It's why you have the role you have. However, being smart means you never stop learning, never stop challenging your assumptions, and never stop looking for better ways.

The Emotion of Disappointment

Emotions give you information. If you're aware of your emotions in real time, it makes you better at your job. For example, if you feel yourself becoming angry, you should be quiet and get away for a break. If you feel charmed, it means you might be talking to a sociopath.

The emotion of disappointment tells you something important: your model about the world is incorrect. Disappointment is when reality and expectations are not aligned. What you expect of the world does not correlate with what is real.

Maybe you were expecting to be given an assignment, or perhaps you were expecting your idea would be embraced by the higher-ups and be implemented. Maybe you expected a potential customer to sign. When these things don't happen, it can be emotionally painful. But most of all, what happens is a lesson. It is a reaction of the world to you and your thoughts, and it is an opportunity to get smarter about what is going on.

The same thing happens when people bring in a new hire to solve a problem. It doesn't always work. They project this person into being the answer, the missing piece, without understanding that work is a system. There's never a magic bullet that fixes an error in a system. People get caught up in the idea, rather than the facts, and then they get disappointed. As a result, the new person is doomed to failure before they begin.

On a personal level, people will behave the way they always behave. We expect new behavior sometimes and are disappointed. We should embrace on the front end that people will behave as they have always behaved.

Knowledge Is Constantly Changing

A few years ago, I was working with the head of engineering for a major international company. During our conversation, he kept telling me how much he knew and what an expert he was. At one point I stopped him and told him that whatever he knew, I could Google. His face turned red. He was not happy. But right when I thought the interaction might go off the rails, he looked up and started to laugh. "You know, you're probably right," he said.

To that I responded with this admission, "I could Google it, but I would have no idea what to do with that knowledge." It's the knowledge in context, not the knowledge itself, that is valuable.

–Joe

I tell medical students that medicine is basically infinite. You can never know everything. Your current knowledge is valuable, but it will be largely obsolete in a decade. What matters more than knowledge is the habit of questioning what you know and updating it. When I was practicing primary care medicine, I used to look things up on the computer right in front of the patient. What's the preferred antibiotic for an ear infection? I think I know, but what if it's changed since the last time I looked it up, or what if I don't remember correctly?

It's the knowledge in context, not the knowledge itself, that is valuable.

–Mike

Moving Beyond the Natural

Step 1: Ask yourself, Does learning and adjusting come natural for me, or is this something I need to improve?

Step 2: How do you handle disappointment? Do you look at it as an opportunity to improve or a statement of failure? Write down some practical ways you might respond to a recent disappointment you have experienced.

Step 3: Because knowledge is constantly changing, take a few moments to think about some assumptions you have not evaluated in some time. Is there new knowledge that could shift the way you think today?

Notes

Maxim 25

TRUST AND RESPECT ARE NONNEGOTIABLES

Trust is not all or nothing. Trust is a spectrum. The amount we trust others changes over time . As situations change, the amount of trust others have in us changes. No one is perfect or without error, and we all sometimes miss the mark or let people down. When this happens, our trustworthiness is in question. At any given time, our personal trust score may be zero in one situation and 100 percent in another.

Trust is not all or nothing.

Some people trust very easily, while others have trouble trusting even those closest to them. So trust might not be the right foundation for building teams. It's not necessarily reliable. It's hard to see or feel compared to other elements that make up a good team. But as Patrick Lencioni notes,

"Teamwork begins by building trust. And the only way to do that is to overcome our need for invulnerability."

Instead, a better starting point is respect. It's much easier to see and feel. Respect is about the way we talk to one another, treat one another, argue, listen, and how we value one another. When respect is in a conversation, we feel valued even when we disagree. With respect, accountability is healthy and helpful.

So how are you ensuring respect is displayed in your organization? Are you checking with others to see how they define respect to ensure the umbrella is broad enough? Do you have a zero-tolerance policy around uncorrected disrespectful behavior? Does your team know this and see you act on it? Are people comfortable letting you know when you begin to come across disrespectfully?

See the Good in Everyone

One of the ways we respect others is by acknowledging the good in them. Benjamin Franklin said that if you want to be popular, you should never say anything bad about anyone. That's a great tip for improving your standing among others. But there's another level to this.

When any two people in conversation tend to start talking about a third person, usually, it doesn't remain positive. Even if they want to avoid gossip and criticism, it still tends to happen. It takes no talent, and it adds no value.

Leadership is the art of overcoming the natural. It's natural to gossip because we are all insecure and fearful. To get past those insecurities, we must cultivate curiosity. When we are curious, judgment is suspended. We can look for the good and avoid the flaws.

Face-to-face, expressing curiosity about others keeps them present and engaged. When judgment shows up, people shut down. They wait to be told what to do rather than show initiative. They keep doing the same thing over and over, even when it isn't working, because they tend not to feel ownership of anything. When people are shut down, they create a negative energy. The entire team now needs to overcome the heavy cloud that lingers overhead. Being curious about people, and appreciating the good you see, makes them lively and creative. How do you feel when people see the good in you and throw praise in your direction?

Anyone can see flaws. But as Mother Teresa said, "If you judge people, you have no time to love them." It takes an unnatural attitude to bring yourself to see people as wonderfully unique, to help them do more of what they do really well, and to thank them for it.

The Benefits of Trusting Culture

I knew a person who created a very large company worth billions of dollars. This man had a difficult time trusting anyone, and life had given him plenty of examples why trust is not always safe. However, I watched as he showed incredible respect to everyone around him. He hired and delegated. He empowered and provided support. He asked questions at the right time and listened in a way that communicated he truly cared. He remembered the little things and honored those who uphold the company's culture.

In the back of his mind, he was listening for inconsistencies or anything that might raise a flag. He had systems and processes in place to ensure things are as they seem, but he truly showed and gave respect freely. The team knew about his trouble with trust, accepted it, and saw it as a challenge to try and earn it little by little. The loyalty he created was off the charts. According to many who place trust as the starting point of a team, this company never could have been built or succeeded. Without respect, that would be true. In spite of the difficulty around trust, respect has driven success.

–Joe

I had a colleague once who was a good leader. However, his supervisor only saw his weaknesses, and no matter how hard this colleague worked, that's all he heard about. I could see him start to give up. You could see it in his body language.

Then he was transferred into a different department where he was highly valued for his insights. He thrived, even when he made mistakes—because they were not seen as something horrible, but something to be learned from and fixed.

–Mike

Moving Beyond the Natural

Step 1: Does trust come naturally for you? If not, write down why you believe this is the case.

Step 2: Take mental inventory of the relationships in your life today. What is one way you could show more trust to those around you?

Step 3: After noting the relationships in your life where you struggle to extend trust, note some creative ways you can work against your natural bent and establish a higher level of respect.

Notes

Maxim 26

BELIEVE IN YOUR TEAM ENOUGH TO SPEAK THE TRUTH

Your team is what you feed it.

For a leader, individual work is not enough. Your job is to inspire other people and motivate groups to work together. To do this, you must build relationships with individuals. You also must understand that most interaction between people in the workplace occurs outside your knowledge or span of control.

Think about your team as a living organism. If you take all the interactions between all the people in the workplace and put them together, something akin to a group mind becomes apparent. The greatest leaders understand that this larger thing can be influenced, inspired, and harnessed for the betterment of the organization.

You can see a microcosm of the social system during the average meeting. Try to see such a gathering as more than just individuals speaking and interacting. A meeting is also a thing unto itself; it is a pattern of interaction. It is like an organism with its own shape, history, and goals. That organism will have biases and assumptions, just like a person. It will have tendencies that are not in the control of the members or the chair. Is it working as efficiently as it can? Where is it going?

Tell the Truth

It's your job to speak the truth at work. By "speaking truth" we mean describing things as you see them, without any modifications. You don't have to be right. You just need to speak your mind.

Speaking the truth is critical for several reasons. First, most systems of ethics indicate that truth-telling has a high value. You have a moral responsibility to speak the truth for the benefit of the group. Second, your organization requires accurate information to be able to react to conditions, to flourish, and to continue to pay you. A line I (Joe) often use with people is "I care too much not to tell you the truth. It doesn't mean I'm right."

Speaking the truth can be painful and disruptive. It's a hard thing to do, but it's not wrong. Doing the hard stuff is what they pay you for, after all. This is not an excuse to use the truth to harm others. To make it easier on them, speak the truth while showing them you care about them. Demonstrate that caring with your eyes, your body language, your openness, your calm voice, and your thoughtful words. You can't sugarcoat it. You just put it out as data while showing you care.

When you have spoken your truth, don't run away. Stay and help them process it. When you're preparing to tell someone a painful truth, others may try to dissuade you. Go ahead and speak that truth. It might be hard, and it might hurt. Remember that you don't own the outcome. If you try to manage how others react, it will get messier. They may laugh and say, "I already know that." They may get angry. They may be devastated over a word choice. That doesn't make it personal. They act like it is, but it's just not.

"In action, watch the timing," as the ancient philosopher Lao Tzu said. Any time you do anything, the likelihood of success will be affected by your choice of the moment to act. You can say anything to anybody if you use the right tone, but you must also have the right timing. There are some days when you can walk into the boss's office and detect a foul mood. That's not the day. Look for the chance.

Share Truth with Kindness

Giving a patient bad news, like telling them they have a terminal disease, never becomes easy. Sometimes it's a shock to the patient, and sometimes you're telling them something they already knew. One of the things a doctor can do to make the interaction better is to stay with the patient afterward. You give them the gift of your time. You sit with them, sometimes in silence, sometimes as they ask you questions, until they are tired of sitting with you and want you to go away. Someone who hears bad news should not be left alone until they are ready.

–Mike

People tend to be more capable of handling information than we think. This was obvious one day when Jennifer called to talk about a situation that was taking place within her team. The team was in a pod arrangement, and one of the new members was extremely talkative. In fact, this person would ask questions over and over throughout the day. The questions weren't bad questions or unreasonable to ask; however, the constant stream was getting in the way of others being able to do their job. Frustration was growing, and people were all talking about this one individual behind her back. When Jennifer called me, she wanted to know how to handle the situation. It seemed complex to her.

I asked a simple but direct question: "If you were that individual everyone was talking about, what would you want?"

There was a moment of quiet followed by a laugh. She said thanks and hung up. A week later she called to say the problem was resolved. She let the individual know what was happening. That person was shocked to find she had been disruptive and had come to an agreement with the team that she would keep a list of questions, and instead of asking them out loud as they came up, she saved her questions until the afternoon break. Within days the team was back to functioning well. Clear, direct communication tends to bring people up rather than break them down.

–Joe

Moving Beyond the Natural

Step 1: Write down the first thing that comes to mind when you hear the word team. Do you think of it as a living organism? Why, or why not?

Step 2: Ask yourself, Do I naturally speak the truth or avoid it?

Step 3: If you speak the truth well, or even if you are just learning, commit to sharing truth with kindness. Go out of your way to be present with others when you share difficult news or feedback.

Notes

Maxim 27

OTHER PEOPLE DETERMINE YOUR LEVEL OF SUCCESS

It's easy to think the important factors in your success are your own intelligence, hard work, education, and drive. Up to a point, that's true.

Yet everything we do as leaders has a social component. Whatever we do, wherever we go, we are connected in some way to the people around us. At work, the social network consists of the people in and around the organization. That network is multidimensional and constantly shifting. More than your own individual efforts, that network will determine whether you succeed. The team you lead and the peers you work with will decide, sometimes consciously and sometimes unconsciously, if they will make you successful or not.

Consider those people in your organization who rally around a project and put in extra time and effort when someone needs help. Think about those people who speak well of their supervisor, engage in problem-solving, and drive results. The leader of these people will likely succeed. Now ask yourself if that level of commitment and drive is uniform across all teams in your organization. Are there some teams whose members roll their eyes when the leader speaks, who work the minimum, and who essentially say, "It's not my problem"?

The people around you will decide whether they will make you successful. It may not be a conscious decision, but it will be based on your engagement, your compassion, and your willingness to make things better. When you speak, do you communicate care and concern for what people are doing? Do people feel trusted and respected by you? Are you open to hearing their ideas and focused enough to be present in the conversation? Are your words and body language communicating the same message, or is there a disconnect?

The people around you will decide whether they will make you successful.

If the answers to these questions are "no," you and your team will likely fail. If people perceive you are trying to advance yourself rather than the team, they will find ways to ensure your success is limited. If you believe your position is what matters, not your behavior, and if you discount relationships and followership, you and your team will likely fail. Likewise, if you speak down to people, do not listen carefully, do not "see" the people around you, and believe you are the smartest person in the room, your team is less likely to invest their own intelligence, energy, and talent in the group's goals.

There are countless examples of organizations where people expelled a leader they did not respect. What we often miss is that while the leader failed, if they had engaged the team differently, the team could have filled the gaps in performance and created success.

Leadership Is Earned, Not Given

After the first sale of a company to a private equity group, the CEO was able to step aside and move on to a new role. Prior to this point, he had been the founder, builder, and energy behind this organization's success. The new owners went on a search for a new CEO and found a person who looked perfect. He possessed a great résumé, great personality, and had great experience.

He entered and came in strong. He made changes, set expectations, and aligned resources. But what he didn't do was build relationships and learn the business. Instead, he continued to live in a town some distance away from where the business was located and became distant and disengaged.

A leadership title does not mean anything if you cannot find a way to win people over and earn their trust and respect.

Within a year, the owners were hearing that the team was not supportive of the new CEO. People were starting to leave. Support dried up. And in a short time, the CEO was replaced. What went wrong? This CEO never understood that leadership was earned, not given.

People make the decision whether you will be successful. A leadership title does not mean anything if you cannot find a way to win people over and earn their trust and respect.

Your Team Determines Your Success

A team's defense against a bad leader is to shut down, withdraw, and hit minimal standards rather than strive for excellence. They will create disharmony and strife and promote a general negative view of the leader. You see this particularly when a team has been in place for a while, and there's a new leader from the outside. The new leader doesn't win the team over, is not open, and talks about the faults of the group. That leader can fail rapidly.

So what are you doing to build a healthy relationship with your team so that they know you care, you value their input and thinking, and you see each person's strengths and not just their flaws? How will you communicate to them that you will do whatever you can, not just to make yourself successful, but them as well?

To succeed, you must set clear boundaries and coach your team into doing the same. You must work with people to help meet expectations. When they win, you must advocate for them, speaking openly outside the group about their great work and individual strengths. When they need correction, you must deliver it in private and with clear criteria for improvement. You must provide opportunities for your people to grow and earn rewards. Promotions, raises, recognition, extra training, and things of this nature will be most meaningful to them. This all creates trust and followership.

The team will work more effectively when they feel they matter and the work they are doing matters. Your job, and your measure of success, is whether they have what they need to succeed.

Why Relationships Are Always the Key

Every leadership position I have had has been offered to me without my seeking it. I was practicing internal medicine when the hospital's previous chief medical officer passed away suddenly. The CEO asked me within a few days if I would consider the position. He said, "I can work with that guy." This may be an uncommon pathway to leadership, but it is a valid one.

–Mike

An organization I was working with brought on a high-level executive. This person was intelligent, had a great work ethic, and brought a world of experience into the new role. Within six months, she was failing. It was painful to watch.

What happened? She came into the role with an expressed attitude of "I am going to show them what they are missing and teach them how to do things right." She didn't take the time to understand how things were being currently done and why. She didn't build relationships and ask questions of those who were already in the organization.

Finally, there was an unrecoverable failure. At an offsite meeting, she presented a new plan that made no sense in the context of the current business strategy. She had not sought input from any of her team in advance. Instead of rallying around her to help, her team just watched her implode. A short while later, she was gone from the organization.

Leadership requires followership and influence, not simply intelligence and experience. Had this individual built relationships, learned about the organization, and brought people on board, there is no doubt she could have added value down the road. The people around her decided if she would be successful. She didn't appear to care, so they didn't care how much she knew.

–Joe

Moving Beyond the Natural

Step 1: Take note of some of the ways others have contributed to the success you have today.

Step 2: Ask yourself, How can I better earn my leadership position?

Step 3: Now, write down several ways you will seek to earn your position this week.

Notes

Maxim 28

SILOS GROW BACK

We cannot live in this world without complex organizations. We wouldn't have cars, houses, or the internet without them. Complex organizations need specialization, and specialization generally means work must be broken up into separate units or departments.

In the department next door, there's always something going on that affects what we're doing over here. Often, though, we're not aware of it until it's too late. This causes friction, inefficiency, and sometimes embarrassment. Silos like this can be thought of as "corporate turfs"—organizational units where people are territorial and defend their work and knowledge from outsiders.

Silos are bad for business because they lead to turf wars, poor communication, and lack of coordination. As such, much work must be done to break them down. Leaders should work against silos to avoid negative outcomes. They should develop relationships and communication channels across departments and divisions and create cross-functional teams.

Working across silos is something you want to do. It makes you a better leader and more valuable to the organization. So get to know people in other departments and divisions. People who know a lot of people can get things done and make better decisions because they have more contexts to work from. Just looking at your immediate work environment and its inputs and outputs is not enough. Get to know people elsewhere and find out what their needs and concerns are. Understand how your team's work and theirs fit together (or don't) in helping the organization achieve its overall goals.

The problem with breaking down silos is that it doesn't last. People are tribal. Whatever group people find themselves in tends to become close-knit. Like a kind of gravity pulling people together, local connections become stronger than the allegiance to the organization. Soldiers will die for their buddies before they die for their country.

As an in-group is created, it creates boundaries to protect itself. Those boundaries become the walls of new silos. So don't expect the silo problem to be resolved. Silos are organic and will keep appearing. The work of breaking down silos is never done.

How to Work Across Silos

> Sometimes, silos are old and have inertia. There's a very old separation in medicine between surgeons and nonsurgeons. There is sometimes mistrust, puzzlement, and even mockery. Having strong relationships across that divide can be useful, but no matter what you do, you're pushing against a force.
>
> *–Mike*

Silos are a term used in the workplace to describe teams that work separately alongside other teams. Over the years many organizations have learned that silos are often not healthy, leading to unnecessary competition and decision-making with insufficient information. For that reason, silos have been broken down in favor of cross-functioning communication and interaction. However, this is easier said than done. Recently I was asked to work with a new organization where the CEO was having difficulty getting the team on board. The team talked about collaboration, but it still wasn't happening. Each would present their own work as if it were perfect, and that was that.

In a meeting I was asked to attend, I threw out a question after one such presentation: "If you were in charge of this project, what would you add, subtract, or do differently?" No one said a word. So I called on someone by name. The conversation started growing, and it finally became apparent that this project was not something the group believed needed to be done. In the silo with limited information, the project appeared sound. But with the entire group's input, it was apparent it failed to fit strategy. What the team learned quickly was that silos were not just structural but part of human nature.

–Joe

Moving Beyond the Natural

Step 1: Identify one area in your company where a silo has emerged.

Step 2: Now, take note of what you think is the root cause of this issue.

Step 3: Write down several steps you will take to break down this silo.

Notes

Maxim 29

DIVERSITY HELPS YOU DEAL WITH UNCERTAINTY

All individuals have limits. You may be extremely intelligent, but that doesn't mean you understand everything from every perspective. You may be an expert in your field, but that doesn't mean you're better at it than everyone else. Doctors, for example, are extremely well trained, but they consult each other about uncertain diagnoses or treatment plans. This doesn't make them less effective; it makes them more effective. Working together helps individual experts do a better job.

The limits of individuals are especially visible when difficult decisions are required, usually with insufficient information. I know that brushing my teeth keeps them healthy, and there is no doubt this is true, so I choose to brush them. It's not an important decision. But deciding whether to get an MBA is a different question. I can't know the exact opportunity cost. I can't know how the contacts I make in school will affect my outlook or my career. I cannot know exactly how much more valuable it will make me. I cannot know how much this choice will affect my income or my family life.

With complete information, the best course of action is usually obvious. Without complete information, we need all the help we can get. We need a variety of people who can see the situation from different perspectives. We need their various kinds of intelligence and intuition.

Abraham Lincoln said that all important decisions are made with incomplete information. He understood that diversity is good for decisions like this. That's why he surrounded himself with people who disagreed with him—the famous "Team of Rivals."

With incomplete information, we need to sort through the uncertainty. We need to find out all the information we can, from whatever corner. We need to think creatively about what might be happening. This process is difficult because acknowledging uncertainty is emotionally uncomfortable. And sometimes we don't understand all the kinds of uncertainties that exist. In a medical diagnosis, for example, there may be uncertainties in the patient's history, in laboratory testing, or in imaging studies. There may also be uncertainties as to the validity of the wisdom handed down through the ages. There may be uncertainty as to the exact definition of the diagnosis, or even the existence of the diagnosis itself.

So in uncertain situations, it's important to have multiple minds working. In your organization, intelligence, knowledge, and skills are distributed, and they must be combined for this to work best. Probably, there is already a certain level of diversity on your team.

How do you harvest the diverse perspectives of your folks? You set up a culture of listening and respecting other people's opinions.

Broaden Your Lens

We all see through a lens that we have developed over the years. Our lenses have served us well, but they are never complete. By changing your circle so it includes many people who are dissimilar to you, you are adding lenses to your mix that have a great upside.

A couple of years ago, I was playing golf with a dear friend. Somehow the conversation turned to young people and policing (my friend is an educator). At one point he looked at me and said, "Joe, you'll never understand what it's like for a black male to be pulled over by a police officer." Over the next couple of hours, he helped my understanding. The more we listen to others who do not look or think exactly like us, the broader our world becomes and the more sensitive we can become to the paths others have walked. The broader our world understanding, the better our chances of navigating uncertain times, transitions, and challenges.

–Joe

Teaching medical residents in Buffalo, I have been exposed to folks from all over the world but mostly Pakistan and India. The intellect of this particular group of people varies as much as any other group of doctors, but some of them have been at least near-geniuses. What a pleasure it has been to talk to them about politics or philosophy for a few minutes here and there during rounds or while on call. A small thought or gesture from them can speak worlds about their background and point of view. I am a better person for seeing things through their eyes briefly and imperfectly. And I think I understand the world and all its uncertainties a bit better.

–Mike

Moving Beyond the Natural

Step 1: Know your limitations. What areas do you especially need the input of others?

Step 2: Think of some ways you could create your own "team of rivals" at your business.

Step 3: List two ways you could harvest the diverse perspectives of others.

Notes

Maxim 30

KNOW WHY YOU'RE MEETING

A common error in our minds is thinking of a meeting as a thing that we go to as individuals. We think about what the meeting must accomplish in terms of our own projects and plans.

This model misses the fact that a meeting is a group process. It's a thing unto itself, sort of like a school of fish, with its own behaviors and directions. A meeting needs constant attention to help it function productively.

When the group is in process, things will happen that no one planned. The group itself will begin to move in unforeseen ways. It may seek to prolong its time together, or to quiet down a certain member, or to defer to a senior person without questioning.

We need to manage these properties of meetings as they emerge. Think about these basic things to start:

What's the Meeting For?

Most meetings are for one of three things: informing, making decisions, or strategizing. If it's for informing, ask someone to send you an email and cancel the meeting. If it's for decision-making, have relevant information sent far enough in advance that participants have time to read and consider, so they arrive at the meeting ready to make good decisions. If the meeting is for strategy, make sure there's enough time, and that the right people are present.

How Long Should It Be?

You usually don't need an hour for a meeting. As the old saying goes, "Work expands to fill the time allotted to it." Why can't the meeting be twenty-five minutes instead of thirty? Rather than making it an hour, cut it to fifty minutes so people have time to go to the bathroom and grab a cup of coffee before their next appointment. This also helps prevent them from being late for their next meeting.

How Many People Should Attend?

If you're solving a problem, have a maximum of six people—preferably fewer. Otherwise, no one will agree in a reasonable time frame. There will just be too many minds to bring together. Larger meetings are good for only two things: informing (which is of questionable marginal value over just an email) and consent. If for consent, format the meeting as a briefing, and if any problems come up, rapidly delegate those to a smaller group at another time. Trying to solve a problem in a room full of fourteen people is a tremendous waste of human capital.

How to Avoid "Overmeeting"

The most common complaint I run across today from executives in all lines of work is that they are constantly in meetings. Meetings tend to show up on calendars with little explanation or purpose. I went to a healthcare technology company in Alabama several years ago. Without exception, everyone on the leadership team had a calendar that was 110 percent full each week with scheduled meetings, and this was based on a fifty-five-hour workweek. What this meant was everyone was working sixty-plus hours a week just in meetings! The group was burned out, and patience was wearing thin. Meetings are important, but they are not your job. Some are necessary, but it's essential to say no to those you don't need to attend and yes to those that come with a relevant agenda and points to consider.

–Joe

If you want a meeting to go well, overprepare. If you have thought everything through beforehand, to the best of your knowledge and ability, you will be ahead of most others and will be able to lead. Years ago, I was asked to chair the credentialing committee of a health insurance company. This committee basically verified that providers were who they said they were and decided whether the organization would contract with certain providers with legal problems. Meetings were hours long when I started. I realized that much of the meeting was spent trying to understand the case. I started preparing all the cases before the meeting, such that I could summarize the facts within a minute or two. This sped up the meetings tremendously. At one point we completed a meeting in twenty-eight minutes.

–Mike

Moving Beyond the Natural

Step 1: Evaluate. What are your meetings like today? Do they start on time? Do they end on time? Do they accomplish what you want them to accomplish?

Step 2: Write down some ways you can make your meetings better.

Step 3: Go back over these tips for running a strong meeting and ask yourself which steps you can implement starting today.

Notes

Maxim 31

YOU SHOULD NOT BE FRIENDS WITH THOSE YOU LEAD

Of all the maxims you will read in this book, this is the one people push back on the most.

Becoming a leader creates separation between you and others. You are no longer one of the buddies on the front line. Owning your role requires maintaining that emotional boundary. No longer can you look for social support at work for your troubles at home. This switch is tough, because this is exactly the kind of thing most people look for at their places of employment, and it's even a predictor of job satisfaction. But as a leader, you must make the switch.

It may seem cold, but we believe you cannot be friends with people at work. Doing so gets in the way of your success and the organization's success. You need friends, people with whom you can show up to their house unannounced, but they should be people who do not work with you. While you might have strong relational ties with some of your coworkers, there should be a clear line in the sand that separates them from your friends who will visit your house on the weekend.

One of the payoffs of this sacrifice is that you have room to be emotionally healthy. After all, being a leader in the workplace means facing hard truths and having hard conversations. Sometimes you will close programs, say no to eager job candidates, and even fire people. It's inevitable. These events are painful enough among acquaintances, but to have them arise among friends can be truly damaging.

But despite the boundaries and separation, leaders can still build close emotional connections. It's just that these connections must have limits. They must be appropriate. Finding this balance is a matter of reflection and of trial and error. The healthiest people know how to go from one conversation to the next, being authentic and genuine while at the same time being appropriate. In almost all relationships, there are topics appropriate to share and ones that should be avoided. Leadership is no exception. At any level of leadership, there are always matters you should not discuss.

So if you find it lonely at the top, you need to ask, "Why am I not looking for better ways to connect?" and "Why am I afraid to open up?" Once the decision to open up is made, just make sure you are opening up about topics that are appropriate, healthy, and valuable. Share the work problems you are struggling with, so your team members understand and help. Only authentic, meaningful relationships allow a team to stay together through difficult struggles and over long periods of time.

One underappreciated benefit of a leadership position is the opportunity to create stimulating work relationships with people you would never meet otherwise. The workplace brings together people from many walks of life. If the organization collects talent, you may find yourself surrounded by tremendously interesting individuals. These relationships can lead you to grow intellectually, professionally, and emotionally in ways that would never happen if, for example, you only socialized with people in your neighborhood or who did the same work you do.

Building Healthy Connections

There is a myth out there that says, "It is lonely at the top." That myth is true when we do not understand roles and boundaries. Everyone needs people to connect with and communicate. For the CEO that becomes a little trickier at times because there are some things that can and cannot be freely shared with the executive team. Transparency does not mean telling people everything that is going on, but it does mean sharing everything necessary for an individual to perform their job.

Take Jasmine, for example. She was new in her role and was trying hard to figure out the right boundaries. What she found was that while there was much she could talk to her team about, there was a different conversation she could have with her board members. In hiring a coach/thought partner, she could have yet another level of conversation. Knowing which conversations to have with which party kept her not only highly connected but also kept her from feeling lonely.

The key is boundaries and knowing which conversations are appropriate with which group. This is very much like parenting, where at times we have very different conversations with young children than we do with a spouse/partner or good friend. Appropriateness is the key.

–Joe

It's unnatural to think this way, but it's useful in a leadership position to separate out your social needs into categories. And many of those categories can be met by the people around you as a leader. So, for example, the need to chat about light topics can easily fit within the boundaries around a leader. Likewise, a game of golf. However, more personal topics such as relationship difficulties or religious beliefs need to be met elsewhere—like at a place of worship or with a counselor.

–Mike

Moving Beyond the Natural

Step 1: Ask yourself, Do I view leadership as lonely?

Step 2: If so, why is this the case?

Step 3: List three boundaries you need to establish with your team to maintain a healthy relational balance.

Notes

Maxim 32

BOUNDARIES SOLVE MORE PROBLEMS THAN WE IMAGINE

Dr. Henry Cloud, author of *Boundaries for Leaders*, said every issue a leader faces is, in fact, a boundary issue. It's hard to find an exception to this rule.

We can define boundaries as emotional, physical, and temporal spaces between two or more people that keep everyone healthy. A boundary might mean a certain kind of behavior is appropriate here but not there; this interpretation of the supervisor's actions is reasonable, but this one is not; or this time of day is for one thing and not for another. Exact boundaries vary widely in different organizations and situations.

You should identify boundaries where they exist and create them where they are needed. Talk about them. Unspoken boundaries lead to misunderstandings, emotional distress, and unnecessary employee discipline. Keeping all parties healthy is the goal.

Our minds and guts let us know when the boundaries are wrong. And the more we learn to listen to ourselves, the more rapidly we start to notice and then adjust our boundaries.

Helpful Boundaries

The following is a list of boundaries we have found helpful.

BOUNDARIES AROUND SAFE COMMUNICATION

Feedback from the boss should not be a surprise. You should be able to speak to your boss without retribution when you see something that concerns you.

BOUNDARIES THAT CREATE A SAFE WORKSPACE

If a coworker is constantly interrupting you, consider saying, "You and I work together really well, but we have different styles. You like to think out loud, but I need to be able to focus. How about we connect in the morning, and at lunch, and at the end of the day, because the constant conversation doesn't work on my end." This is a boundary in a shared space.

BOUNDARIES AROUND WORKLOAD

If someone isn't carrying their load and is putting extra burden on coworkers, this creates resentment. There should be an ongoing conversation here, defining the boundary of what each person should do and measuring actions against that standard.

BOUNDARIES AROUND BEHAVIOR

Remember, whatever is happening around you is because you allow it. If people are being disrespectful, the truth is you are allowing them to be disrespectful. If people are coming in late, this is because you have taught them it doesn't really matter. If people are asking you to solve their problems, you have not taught them how to do their job. Is there an individual that you are allowing to underachieve? Is there someone not aligned with the team or organizational goals? These are not simply performance issues; these are all boundary issues.

Whatever is happening around you is because you allow it.

BOUNDARIES BETWEEN PERSONAL AND PROFESSIONAL LIFE

This is not an easy balance to strike, but it is important. Some people are comfortable sharing everything, and some very little. This makes it hard to construct a space where everybody feels healthy. The core focus should be on allowing people to connect in a meaningful way. What is it about you that would help others feel they know you in appropriate ways? What is it about others that if you knew it, it would help them feel "seen" as individuals? This is where boundaries start.

DISCUSSING POLITICAL AND RELIGIOUS FRUSTRATIONS AT WORK IS RARELY USEFUL

Discussing personal health problems is also rarely useful. Complaining about the boss, a coworker, bills, or finances all cause unnecessary drama. What's the need? Does it uplift and encourage, or just take up time and energy? And then there's the boss who feels lonely and begins to form inappropriate relationships at work, including romances. Nothing good for the business can come out of this type of behavior.

Boundaries around Feedback

I try to make a boundary around feedback to me to make it safe. One way I do this is to thank people for telling me when I'm wrong. In fact, for a while it was my policy to give a gift card to anyone at work who tells me I'm wrong about anything.

–Mike

A supervisor was having trouble connecting with his employees. He had had difficult relationships in his past, and life had taught him relationships were fraught with danger and he was better off staying as far away from personal interactions as possible. But his team felt he was totally disconnected and didn't care.

It turned out he had an outlet for the pain he had been through—creating works of art. The art was fantastic. Ultimately, he agreed to bring in photos of his art and post one on his desk every week or so. People noticed, and conversations began. They were safe conversations. His team talked about his art, not his relationships. His team then started talking about their own hobbies and interests.

The shift in team dynamics was priceless. People started to understand more and more about the supervisor, and he started to connect more and more with the team. Performance improved as did morale. Together, they found a way to connect that kept all parties healthy.

–Joe

Moving Beyond the Natural

Step 1: Evaluate the boundaries you have. Are they satisfactory, or are the lack of boundaries in your life creating challenges?

Step 2: Categorize the key relationships in your life today.

Step 3: Now, write down what your boundaries need to be for this relationship.

Notes

Maxim 33

FRIENDLY IS BETTER THAN FRIENDS

You may not like this one, but we must tell it as we see it. Work is where people spend the most time outside their homes, and it's natural to make friends there. Friendships make work more pleasant and more satisfying. In a true friendship, though, the connection is deep, and boundaries come down. We relax and say exactly what is on our mind. In a work relationship, these conversations cloud judgment and create the appearance of favoritism.

Some people can, among friends, still be objective, make hard decisions, and take unpleasant actions. But this is a rare ability, and your team may not believe you are objective. This is a risk.

Friendship among coworkers can also become a problem for the working unit. For example, in a hospital, nurses on a given floor can become very good friends with each other. When problems come up in the way the floor functions, the network of friendships becomes so strong that the culture of the work unit cannot be changed. Sometimes, the only way to correct the problem is to relocate or eliminate the bulk of the people in such a unit and start again from scratch—an unpleasant and time-consuming solution that is best avoided.

So workplaces tend to function better without close friendships. This principle runs against our natural tendencies, and it may be hard to accept. Thus, say to yourself, "This person next to me is my acquaintance but not my best friend." Such boundaries define an emotional space that allows everyone to stay healthy. Unfortunately, we usually learn where those boundaries should be by making mistakes. If the leader's boundaries are healthy, the people around the leader stay healthy, and their relationships stay appropriate.

On the other hand, everyone deserves friendliness. If there is someone you don't like, who triggers your shadow side, who reminds you of that bad breakup in your past or the kid who tormented you on the playground, make a special effort to be friendly toward that person. Spend more time with them until you can see them as a unique human being. There is no worse feeling in a workplace than knowing one is shunned by a leader, and that everyone is aware of it.

Keeping friendship out of the workplace involves an important balance, because we must have emotional connections in the workplace, but connections that still allow for some separateness.

Why do we need emotions at work at all? First, emotions make connections durable. For example, a strong feeling of mission can hold a team together over time, even though the team members are not friends. This is in contrast to a purely transactional connection, which might occur with somebody who is just there for a paycheck or a line on their résumé. Second, an emotional connection allows for more breadth of communication between two people. The emotional tone of an interaction adds a dimension that makes context and meaning easier to understand.

Leaders should have friendships outside the workplace. Leaders need to have a place where they can relax their boundaries and say things without worrying about the consequences. Even if you move into a new town where you don't know anyone, you can find social outlets outside of work. No matter how small the town is, there will be people who don't work there.

The idea that "friendships" at work are counterproductive may be wrong or may be partly right. We are just suggesting that it might be worth some thought.

Friend or Friendly?

When I was young, I was obsessed with authenticity. I thought everyone should just "be themselves." In fact, I had some distaste for professionalism. Why should people be closed off and artificial? Wasn't that a way of being dishonest? As I have grown older, I have come to appreciate professionalism. There are many kinds of people who come to the workplace or marketplace. Each person has their own particularities, and not everyone will enjoy everyone else. Professionalism is a way to smooth off some of the rough edges we each have, so that we are ready to talk to other people who might be quite different from us. It's a way to keep from scaring each other.

–Mike

I had been working with a certain organization for about seven years, and while speaking to a group I brought up the "friend" versus "friendly" distinction. When I mentioned that leaders shouldn't have friends in the workplace, the hands shot up. People were making comments such as, "We thought you understood us, and now it's apparent you don't," and "Your values and our values are not aligned. We don't know where you got this from, but it makes us question our work over the years." They yelled at me and all but ran me out of the room. That was October. They brought me back in May to talk about the intervening period. It had been eventful. A supervisor had taken his reports out to a bar, and the supervisor received a DUI. Another supervisor was sleeping with an employee. It was a huge mess. This time, they intentionally wanted to discuss "friend" versus "friendly."

–Joe

Moving Beyond the Natural

Step 1: Ask yourself, Do I agree with Joe and Mike's assessment that leaders should not be friends with those they lead?

Step 2: Evaluate the relationships you have in your workplace. Are they healthy, or have you allowed yourself to grow too close to those you lead?

Step 3: Take note of your work culture. How does your team interact with one another? Are friendships resulting in a decrease in productivity?

Notes

Maxim 34

YOU ARE PAID NOT TO AVOID CONFLICT

Conflict is inevitable in business. It happens any time people are working together. It is a natural, healthy, and normal feature of any kind of relationship. As you are probably already aware, there are healthy and unhealthy ways to handle conflict.

Many people find themselves in the business world with unhealthy habits learned from their families. They had poor role models. When something wasn't right, somebody yelled, withdrew, or both. Those patterns are destructive in a work environment.

Many people avoid conflict by avoiding the truth. They tell people what they want to hear, rather than what needs to be said. The goal becomes, *How do I please people at this moment?* This is never a good strategy. At work, everyone needs to understand what is real.

If you care about other people at work, be direct with them. Ultimately, being honest and confronting when necessary is the best way to please others. "You're failing right now. How can I help you?" This doesn't mean you should be rude or brutal in the way you handle the truth. Think it through, write out what you want to say, rehearse it, and then deliver the message with a smile.

A Practical Approach to Conflict

When conflict arises, step back and take time for reflection. Ask yourself where the conflict is coming from. If you act without reflection, your emotions can consume the situation, your logic becomes weak, and the conflict can grow out of control.

As you reflect, ask yourself exactly what is bothering you. Is your reaction due to a difference of opinion? Or is it in response to a personal value that is threatened? Are you reacting to experiences you had in the past, either with this individual or others? Is your reaction due to a real or perceived injury to you or someone else?

Once the source of your reaction has been identified, start asking questions. Say, "Tell me more," and then listen carefully, without expressing yourself. The other person can then expand the story that is being created in their minds. The story of the other person is important information.

What you don't want to do is make up a story without information. You don't want to make false inferences. The best way to do this is to ask questions and listen.

Repeat back what the other person is saying, using active listening, until the story builds in your mind. "This is what I hear you saying . . ." This should be iterative until the repeating back is acknowledged as accurate.

Once that confirmation is achieved, it is critical to respond with "I" statements. For example, "When you correct me in front of the team, I feel disrespected and incompetent." This technique helps keep the emotion at the same level, without escalating. It also gives us the opportunity to express what we think, feel, believe, and need. "You" statements tend to escalate the conflict.

At this point, after learning what the other has said, and after making "I" statements, stop and take a read of the other person. Where are they? Ideally, when you speak calmly and clearly around your needs and thoughts, you will be able to bring the other person to a calmer and clearer place, where both parties can engage in dialogue. Agreement isn't necessarily the goal, but clear communication is.

There are times when the other party will not be calm. At that point, pause the conversation to allow both parties to breathe and relax, and return to the conversation later. Alternatively, simply reach the resolution of agreeing to disagree.

Some Handle Conflict Better Than Others

Watching college basketball is a passion of mine. I enjoy the intensity—watching the teams play their hearts out. One thing I notice is that the coach is constantly in the ear of the best players, giving feedback in a very strong and direct way. And the players are eating it up. Why? Because they know they can improve and that the coach genuinely has their best interest in mind. In the same way, leaders who have genuine care for their employees deliver feedback at a high rate.

–Joe

I have had hundreds of conversations in intensive care units with families of dying patients. People come in from out of town for such emergencies, and family conflict will come to the surface. For example, a daughter has been living two thousand miles away and feels guilty she has not been there. A son has chosen to stay in the hometown to take care of the aging parent, and has been doing so every day for years, and feels resentful of his sister. Multiple unspoken factors can be present: the daughter's guilt urges her to demand aggressive medical care, and the son identifies with the suffering of the parent feeling the time has come to "let go." The only way out of these situations, and many similar ones, is talking. "Tell me about what you think is going on," I would ask, and give time for each relative to speak their mind, to be fully heard. Only after that will they listen. You can't just walk into an ICU and give a pronouncement about what you think and expect it to be effective. You must actively listen.

–Mike

Moving Beyond the Natural

Step 1: Ask yourself, How well do I handle conflict?

Step 2: Take note of any conflicts you currently have in your life.

Step 3: Write down one way you will confront a conflict in your life this week.

Notes

Maxim 35

IF YOU DON'T AGREE WITH YOUR BOSS, HIDE IT

When a supervisor brings you into a conversation about new ideas, sometimes their suggestions make perfect sense and are easy to support. Sometimes, however, their ideas appear ridiculous. At this point, it's time to stop and listen.

Remember, the person with the idea has spent time thinking about it. So ask for more information. And after listening, the idea may not seem logical or practical. And if so, it's OK to respectfully push back at this point and look for more clarification. At some point, if you have pushed back and still don't agree, what do you do now? Now you must accept.

By accepting, you acknowledge that those above you have a vantage point you might not. They have more information, and it is their decision to make. No one should be able to tell which one you are doing: agreeing or accepting. That's the best way to support your organization. You model good behavior and avoid drama.

No matter which you choose, you must not publicly disagree with leadership, or passive-aggressively work against the idea. That would be sending the message that leadership is not competent. Remember, your boss is not paying you for sabotage.

The "agree or accept" principle changes your life at work. It keeps your side of the street clean. It prevents you from becoming the reason something didn't work. It leaves the possibility that people know things you don't know. It makes you a positive force, rather than neutral or negative.

If you don't have full enthusiasm about an idea, but you support it anyway, keep in mind your opinion could easily be wrong. Very frequently, ideas we think are foolish can work out well.

If your supervisor will not allow you to ask questions or will not take the time to give you information when needed, it is most likely time to look for a new place to work. The same applies if you are asked to accept anything that is illegal, immoral, or just plain wrong. These situations are extremely rare but do happen on occasion.

Hide Your Disagreements

While having a healthy discussion with your boss is essential for alignment and clarity, hiding disagreement once you leave the office is a skill to be developed. When we hide our disagreement, we are saying, "I don't see it, but I trust you; let's give it a shot." When we don't hide our disagreement, we are saying, "This person is not as smart as I am, so I'll just go through the motions." One is a position of respect and awareness, and the other is a position of arrogance and immaturity.

–Joe

When Microsoft Windows was released in the 1990s, I thought it was a poor idea. Why can't people just remember the commands? Pull-down menus were a waste of time and made you lazy. It made you further away from the machine. I told people around me in my organization exactly how I felt. Effectively, it was low-grade sabotage. Obviously, I was wrong, and like the rest of the world, I benefit from this kind of user interface every day.

–Mike

Moving Beyond the Natural

Step 1: Write one to three areas in which you differ from your supervisor.

Step 2: Now, consider which, if any, of these you might want to share with them.

Step 3: After this discussion, work hard to hide your areas of disagreement.

Notes

Maxim 36

ASK YOURSELF WHAT YOU ARE MISSING BY NOT THINKING

Workplaces can be chaotic. It's possible to spend the whole day responding to legitimate, important concerns, brought to you by earnest people, without spending a minute on the core mission of the business or the key relationships necessary for the business to function. It's possible to ignore major problems when one is caught up in this kind of reaction. Common sense may not function at all.

People in leadership roles must find a way to stay out of the chaos and find time to think. It's their job. It is crucial for the business, and all employees who depend on it for their livelihood, for leaders to have uninterrupted time to think things through. *How is my team working together? Where are people struggling? Who are the people who are looking to take on more?* It's also the job of leaders to notice what is occurring outside the organization, and how it might need to change for the future. "Thinking" can be making the rounds and talking to people, reading, verifying data, or journaling.

In modern workplaces, there is a huge preoccupation with looking busy. When we're thinking, it doesn't look like we're doing anything. As a leader, you must get beyond your insecurity about the judgment of others who might think you are not working as hard as them.

Even beyond the executive level, a supervisor or manager must have thinking time. If the supervisor isn't thinking, are the frontline workers themselves really thinking? Anybody who is managing a group of people and processes must have time to think.

The Importance of Thinking

A CIO I worked with in the early 2000s started off as the second employee of a home care agency in North Carolina. The company did very well and went into a growth mode, acquiring multiple other home health businesses. As the company grew, the CIO's role was to integrate all the information systems. His job was not only to keep all the business units running but to create an information system that would work far into the future, without limiting growth.

At that time, technology was exploding. If you were not reading and learning, there's no way you could be on the front end of it. This CIO had a hard time giving himself permission to sit at his desk and learn. He felt awkward because it looked like he wasn't doing anything. Yet there was probably nothing better for him to do than sit at his desk reading trade magazines.

Leaders aren't used to that. There's a part of us that feels guilty, without understanding that the job is to think and learn and question. Time spent on those pursuits is not only valid work but essential work.

–Joe

It's hard to figure out whether you're actually thinking. If you're comfortable, chances are you're not. There is nothing comfortable about real thinking. Thinking involves turning the mind aggressively to the things demanded by the situation. That process should not stop just because the circumstances make you uncomfortable or because the results of the thinking make you uncomfortable. In fact, those are exactly the situations where one must persevere with thinking, if one is to understand reality. And understanding reality is essential for organizational function.

–Mike

Moving Beyond the Natural

Step 1: Ask yourself, *Where do I think best?*

Step 2: Now, create margin in your calendar to think.

Step 3: Include your team in the discussion and give them room to think and make suggestions.

Notes

Maxim 37

JUDGE LEADERS BY HOW THEY PROMOTE OTHERS

Great leaders produce other great leaders. If you want to find great leaders, look for people who have made others succeed.

This is a key test of leadership. Think about Oprah Winfrey and Martha Stewart. They both have personal brands and many business successes. Yet Oprah has created multiple successful people through her work. Martha, not so much. As Sheryl Sandberg notes, "Leadership is about making others better as a result of your presence, and making sure that impact lasts in your absence."

What if your organization had the following policy? *No one is promoted beyond first-line supervisor without considering how many people they have gotten promoted.* How many line workers did this supervisor get promoted to supervisor? With this criterion for moving up the ladder, supervisors know it's important to develop their people.

Under such a policy, people everywhere in the organization would understand they share a primary responsibility to develop the people around them. Morale and loyalty would improve because people would know they are respected, trusted, and valued. People who are just good at self-promotion would not get promoted. It might even be a protective measure against promoting sociopaths.

Make no mistake, such a policy would be disruptive. Some would get left behind because making other people shine is not in their skill set. Some would leave the organization rather than learn the skills they lack. But it would be worth it.

How does your organization handle it when key people leave? If someone leaves the organization for a bigger opportunity, it's not a betrayal. It's a compliment. You can congratulate yourself that your leadership worked—and created an opportunity for the next emerging leader.

Who Are You Promoting?

I have a world of respect for Oprah Winfrey and all she has done, achieved, and created. For me the thing that most sets her apart from so many others of our time is the enormous number of people she has promoted. Leaders make others better. Leaders highlight the achievements of others, and in my mind no one has done this better than Oprah. If you want to find a true leader today, look at the number of people they have built up, promoted, and assisted along their journey.

–Joe

If it's your project to make people around you better, you must be ready for them to outshine you. And then you must decide how much you want to advertise that you helped them succeed. These are tough situations. My philosophy is to make a few comments about the help I provided but otherwise to sit back and let the leader take the spotlight.

–Mike

Moving Beyond the Natural

Step 1: Do some self-evaluation. Do you focus more on getting a promotion than promoting others?

Step 2: Write down one or two creative ways you could elevate those below you on the org chart.

Step 3: Reframe the way you view people's departure from your team. If there are problems, fix them. But if people are leaving because you have empowered them to be greater leaders, be encouraged.

Notes

Maxim 38

YOUR JOB IS TO MAKE YOUR BOSS LOOK GOOD

Your boss has an essential function in the organization. They will succeed when they do their job well. When you help your boss succeed, and be seen to succeed, you are helping the organization. The organization signs your paycheck. Therefore, it is the moral thing to do: make your boss successful, and therefore make your boss look good.

Apart from practical functions, bosses have a symbolic function. They must be seen as trustworthy, competent, and caring—like any other leader. To the extent you can help your boss display those characteristics, you are helping the organization, and you are doing your job thereby.

"No one is a hero to their valet," as the saying goes. You are likely aware of the dark side of your boss's personality, of their faults, weaknesses, and moments of confusion. This changes nothing. Your boss's outtake reels are not what the organization should be seeing.

On the other hand, if you sabotage the people above you, you damage the organization. You have a moral reason not to do that, because you're not working for free. You may decide you don't want to be there anymore, but you must not hurt the place you work.

Likewise, if there is a decision or a policy you don't agree with, you need to accept it (or decide it's time to move on). You cannot be seen not to support your boss or the organization.

Let's say your boss has a new idea on Monday morning. She explains it, and you don't understand. "Tell me more," you say. You dialogue about it. After you ask all your questions and raise all your doubts, she still believes this is the best decision. At that point, you must agree or accept—and whichever you decide to do, do it in such a way that no one can tell which you chose.

Your disagreeing with the boss doesn't mean the boss is wrong. Sometimes, people with crazy ideas are brilliant and their ideas work. The boss, after all, sees things at a different level, and it's their decision. And assuming their decision is not immoral and does not break the law, it is up to us to carry out those decisions.

People do not hire you to make their lives more difficult. People hire you because they believe you will help move the company forward and add to the team in positive ways and support the agenda they are driving.

People do not hire you to make their lives more difficult. People hire you because they believe you will help move the company forward and add to the team in positive ways and support the agenda they are driving. It is our job to lead upward, meaning to help our boss be as successful as possible so that they are informed, prepared, and able to put their best foot forward.

Why Undercutting a Boss Never Ends Well

"Agree or accept" has always been a problem for me. I was raised to be an independent thinker, and if I don't think something's a good idea, it's hard for me to hide it. I've had to work at it, but I have learned to suspend my judgment inside organizations because organizations can have complex systems of wise decision-making that I can't see into. The need for this approach became clear during my years as the chief medical officer of a small hospital. Every week I would watch the decision-making process of the senior leadership team. They would be juggling multiple factors, including some that could not be announced publicly; examples would be details about specific patients or human resources issues with an individual employee. The decisions were generally wise, but the underlying basis of the decisions could not be shared with the staff or community.

–Mike

Time and time again, I have seen situations where someone undercuts their boss, and it doesn't end well. When I first got out of seminary, I was in contact with several classmates. We were all out there trying to learn our role, adapt to the pressures, and apply our academic learning to the practical side of working with people.

One friend called, and the excitement in his voice was clear. The leaders of the congregation were not happy with the senior pastor and were trying to see how they might remove him. From all I was told, this had come down to personalities, and the senior pastor was losing the battle. My friend joined in with the group who was working to remove his boss. I remember thinking, "This sure sounds unhealthy and dangerous." Irrational power struggles typically don't just go away once a battle has been fought.

The senior pastor was removed (not at all easy to do, but he was basically run out), and my friend was promoted to his role. Eight months later a new struggle emerged with the same group, and my friend was expelled. Becoming a wedge between the organization and your boss is never healthy. It demonstrates a lack of integrity. Generally, it ends poorly. If your boss wins, everyone wins. By supporting your boss, speaking well of them, helping them out, you can calm the organization, add stability to the ranks below, and learn from the person you support.

–Joe

Moving Beyond the Natural

Step 1: Ask yourself, Why was I hired to do my job?

Step 2: Now, consider the ways you are advancing your boss's agenda. Are you more interested in charting your own path, or are you more focused on helping others?

Step 3: Identify any areas you might be pushing against those in leadership above you and realign your perspective to match their ideals.

Notes

Maxim 39

DON'T LET YOUR INTELLIGENCE BE DEVILISH

Intelligence is powerful and useful in many circumstances. But it's not the only thing needed, and many personal factors also contribute to success. These include self-discipline, emotional intelligence, and being a "team player."

For several reasons, high intelligence can create mistrust. First, intelligence is located in an individual, not spread across a group, so it may not be controllable by institutional forces. Remember, people always have shadow sides, and they can easily have hidden motives. Any intelligent person perceived to have hidden motives can easily create suspicion and fear.

Second, intelligence does not necessarily protect you from having bias. Biases impair our ability to figure out what's real or not, and intelligent people can be filled with them.

Third, and most significantly, intelligent people sometimes ignore reality altogether. To paraphrase the medieval Islamic philosopher Ibn

Khaldun, intelligent people don't try to make their thinking conform to reality, but rather ignore facts and treat their thoughts as reality. Reality is always much more complex than any map we make of it.

To avoid being an intelligent but mistrusted team member, continually focus on the organization's best interests. Demonstrate positivity. Speak frequently of "the good of the organization." Make it clear that your intelligence—along with your energy, caring, and other qualities—is dedicated to the betterment of the group. Examine yourself carefully for even the appearance of undermining or undoing the work going on around you.

If you have a spiritual discipline, such as prayer or meditation, bring this resolve into that discipline so your shadow side can be aligned with the rest of you. Be aware of your own mistakes, admit them to others, and seek feedback so that when you start to step off the correct path, others will tell you.

Without such demonstrations of dedication and openness, intelligent or otherwise talented individuals may also appear as *personal* threats to the current leaders of the organization.

When Devilishness Gets the Better of Us

I was asked to work with a medical group that was going through changes. As I started working with the doctors and support team, I found them to be focused and committed and yet somewhat naive around how their own business worked. As I spent time with the CEO and listened to what he was saying and then listened to the team, there appeared to be a disconnect. The CEO was brilliant with a very sharp mind. Within a short period of time, I had the impression the CEO was talking to everyone about playing checkers, while at the same time he had a hidden chess game being played out in the background. As I became more uncomfortable, I made the decision to exit the project.

A year later the practice was sold, the CEO walked away with a large check, and the members of the group all received relatively small checks. But no one was happy, and no one wanted to stay in the new group that had purchased them. Over the next year, as several folks called me to talk and discuss options, what I heard repeatedly was "This was not what we thought we had agreed to," and "How did we not understand what he (the CEO) was doing?" Intelligence is essential in today's world; however, when intelligence is used in devilish ways, the damage is frightening.

–Joe

Some people rely heavily on unquestioned ideas. You can think about these as dogmas or ideologies. These are convenient because they make the world clear. However, they are oversimplifications. For people who cling to them, a questioning intelligence will appear to be devilish.

–Mike

Moving Beyond the Natural

Step 1: Think of a situation where your intelligence in an area created distrust.

Step 2: Now, be honest with yourself and ask if there was anything you could have done differently to create more trust?

Step 3: Keep your intelligence in check. Prevent it from being devilish by continuously supporting the broader mission of your organization.

Notes

Maxim 40

BE THE CEO OF YOURSELF

You own your career and your personal development. Your workplace may or may not be focused on developing its people. Either way, you are responsible for knowing and building your options for the future.

One way to do this is to maximize your value to the organization now. Take these steps to set you apart, solidify your position, and optimize your flexibility for the future.

Every few days, ask your supervisor, "What can I do today to help you the most?"

Every month, ask your supervisor, "What am I not doing the way you want me to, and how does it need to look?" These questions invite feedback in a way that is nonthreatening. You are opening a door.

After you ask these questions, stay in the conversation until you are given something tangible to act on. Don't let them say "nothing." Then it's imperative that you act on that data and correct whatever issue has arisen. The supervisor may now feel they can discuss problems with you without hurting your feelings.

Every six months, sit down with your supervisor or their supervisor and ask, "In order to move forward in the organization, can you please let me know what skill would be most helpful for me to develop?" Again, stay engaged until you have a data point that is actionable. The reason it's every six months is that a skill takes time to develop. Once the point is shared, you need to plot out a self-development plan for that new skill. As you develop that skill, ask if there is a project that would allow you to practice it while it is being developed.

Supervisors almost never hear these questions from their employees. These questions open dialogue, establish a comfortable level of honesty, and remove blind spots and awkwardness. For the individual, the answers provide data that can be used to map out development in the most productive way.

We don't automatically know what actions and skills will maximize the function of our work unit and our organization. If we act on that information, we will be more likely to be retained in the event of a layoff and be better prepared if we are not.

These are the things we can control in a world full of change and disruption. We focus on what we can do. We stay away from passivity and go into an action mode. In moving forward, challenges don't feel so overwhelming, and our sense of control is more rooted in ourselves than in the organization.

Own Your Career

One of the biggest lessons young leaders need to learn quickly is to own their own career. Years ago, Herman Cain wrote a book entitled *CEO of Self*. The title conveys a powerful message. Do not let anyone else oversee your career. Be proactive and make sure you are driving your career in the direction you want it to go.

–Joe

Professionals from technical fields—like doctors and engineers—may not be so good at executive-level planning of their careers. We spend our days wrestling with a volume of specific technical details, and such thinking is quite different from the executive thinking necessary to progress through a community of others.

–Mike

Moving Beyond the Natural

Step 1: List several ways you are increasing your self-development.

Step 2: Every few days, ask your supervisor, "What can I do today to help you the most?"

Step 3: Every month, ask your supervisor, "What am I not doing the way you want me to, and how does it need to look?"

Notes

Maxim 41

DON'T SOLVE YOUR TEAM'S PROBLEMS

Micromanagement replaces your team's best thinking with your thinking.

If you are personally solving urgent problems, you're not holding your people accountable. Urgent problems mean the workplace is getting out of control, and if things are getting out of control, someone isn't doing their job. It may be because they don't know how to do it, or because they need someone to make them do it, or because they don't believe they have the authority, or because they are not a good fit for the organization. Whatever the reason, there is no accountability at the level of the urgent problem, and someone is letting it happen.

Let's say there are some directors who are not playing well together, and the conflicts become acute. For the CEO to address the problem herself is to address the symptom. The problem is really the vice presidents who manage the directors. They are not being held accountable to create cooperation.

As the leader, an *urgent* problem is not *your* problem. Your challenge is figuring out at what level of the organization the fire is and getting the correct person to solve it. Your job is remaining the calm, cool center of the crisis. Your job is continuing to think and be objective, and to see the context.

Somewhere below you in the organization is the person with the greatest firsthand knowledge of the situation. That person may not be an executive, or even a manager. Find this person, the one with the most expertise, and give them authority to solve the problem. Doing so means you must step back, avoid getting personally involved, and let the expert use their knowledge.

Your job is not to dive in and solve the problem yourself. That's a trap that executives get caught in constantly. Note that diving in to solve a problem isn't the same thing as a "deep dive." A deep dive is to check the effectiveness of the leaders around you, not to solve their problems. If I manage you, I do a deep dive so that I have context around my ideas of how well you are doing.

Here's why things get worse if you solve the problem yourself. First, you're bypassing and therefore weakening the organization's structure and lines of accountability. This means you are feeding the chaos. And chaos is the opposite of a well-ordered structure.

You're making people feel incompetent and not allowing them to grow. For an organization to function well, leaders below you and their teams need to solve their own problems. This way, they will be more likely to prevent them and less likely to create more drama. Also, if you solve the problem, the person with expertise doesn't get a chance to impress you.

You're still not going to have the truth. You'll gather a sliver of the truth, but that doesn't mean you have your hands around the situation. Other people will have other slivers of the truth, and in the end the people doing the actual work will have a better picture of what's going on than you ever will. Defer to expertise. Don't replace your team's best thinking with your one-off thinking. Let them know it's their job to handle it.

If you solve the problem yourself, now you're incompetent. You're not leading the organization correctly. You're not drawing lines of accountability. You're undermining the authority of the people who report to you. These are not the actions of a competent leader.

Your team can now blame you if something goes wrong. If you, based on your incomplete knowledge of the situation, come up with a solution and it doesn't work as well as it could, that makes you look bad.

If you solve the problem, you won't see how good your team is at solving it, or which individuals might be good candidates for promotion to problem-solving roles.

You're now creating an opportunity cost. If you spend your mental bandwidth on a crisis, you are not monitoring and managing other parts of the organization, your mind has no time to assess and manage external threats, and so on. This kind of distraction is bad for the organization's health. You may have the power and latitude to dive down and ignore your other responsibilities for a while, but that doesn't mean it's the right thing to do.

People like fires because they are dramatic. People get to be heroes in a crisis, and it's much more fun than smooth day-to-day operations. But it's not as good for the organization. Don't reinforce the drama, and don't go to the rescue. Get the experts to solve the problem, then focus on prevention.

You Need to Develop Those Below You

Doctors are control freaks. We are taught from the beginning that anything that happens or doesn't happen is our fault. You're an intern and the labs weren't drawn today? Go draw them yourself. The paperwork wasn't done for the MRI? Do it yourself and wheel the patient downstairs. Every single detail must be checked, rechecked, and verified. Every loop must be closed, because every other person in the hospital may not know what they are doing, or may forget, or may be lazy. Unfortunately, this kind of attitude toward one's work does not easily lend itself to healthy delegation. In the end, this "hero" role is not sustainable. It's better to create systems that prevent and catch errors. Then the benefit accrues to all the patients, not just yours.

–Mike

There's a story about Thomas Watson, the founder of IBM. One of his executives made a million-dollar mistake and was called in. "I'm sure you called me in to dismiss me," the executive said.

Watson said, "Why would I fire you? I just spent a million dollars to educate you."

–Joe

Moving Beyond the Natural

Step 1: Remember, urgent problems are not your problem.

Step 2: Consider a situation you face today and are tempted to step in and fix it.

Step 3: List some ways you can avoid "going to the rescue."

Notes

Maxim 42

SUCCESSFUL PEOPLE THRIVE ON ACCOUNTABILITY

Sometimes a leader, especially someone who is new to their role, will feel uncomfortable holding others accountable for the work they should be doing. Moving up to leadership from the rank and file, the leader will remember the camaraderie of his or her prior work group and hold back from becoming the bad guy, taskmaster, or disciplinarian. Unfortunately, giving in to this temptation can hurt the organization.

Leaders in an organization are paid to do this job. And if they are avoiding this responsibility, they are in the wrong. The organization needs someone to make sure things get done, and that people are doing what they are supposed to do. That's you. It's hard, but that doesn't make it wrong. Remember, you're paid to do the hard stuff.

Successful people appreciate being held accountable. As Maya Angelou once said, "I do my best because I'm counting on you counting on me." No one is free of blind spots, and sometimes it takes the boss to show them that what they are doing is not exactly in line with what they should be doing. People who are responsible and work hard will appreciate honest and constructive feedback. Workers in some organizations can go a really long time without any meaningful feedback. Don't let that happen. Hold them accountable.

Feedback and accountability don't have to mean you're the bad guy. If you provide the feedback with warmth and compassion, the truth will be easier to accept. Your words and actions should convey this message: "I care about you too much not to tell you the truth."

Earn the Right

Why did Michael Jordan always take the last shot when the game was on the line? The answer is he earned the right. Accountability is not about being under someone's thumb or about blame. Accountability is about earning the right. When we are young, we often beg our parents to let us do something that seems special: cutting the lawn, watching a younger sibling, helping to cook dinner. And we promise to do what we say we are going to do. This is where accountability starts.

–Mike

Recently, I was with a group when I asked what I thought was a very simple question: "Who in this room of leaders loves being accountable?" Much to my surprise, only a few people raised their hands. Accountability and leadership go hand in hand. Accountability is about being counted on, not being perfect, but doing what we say we are going to do when we say we are going to do it. If you don't like accountability for any of several reasons—stress, pressure, or not wanting to be on the hook—then you don't want to be in a leadership position.

–Joe

One of the key predictors of whether someone will be a good doctor is the ability to work with others and accept feedback. I call this "absence of a personality disorder." Doctors are trained to be individualistic and self-sufficient, but in reality, medicine is a team sport, and you can't practice modern Western medicine without a system around you. To work within that system, you need to be able to self-correct. When data on your performance comes in, you need to improve yourself. Good medical students and residents understand this, and when you correct them or offer constructive feedback, they say "thank you." Whenever I see someone get offended and withdraw or argue, I start to worry.

–Mike

Moving Beyond the Natural

Step 1: Ask yourself, Do I struggle to keep people accountable?

Step 2: Evaluate how your previous work positions have shaped the way you hold people accountable today.

Step 3: Remember that true care for others means you love them enough to tell them the truth.

Notes

Maxim 43

WHEN PEOPLE DON'T DO WHAT THEY SHOULD, THEY PROBABLY DON'T KNOW HOW

Don't assume your team knows everything you do. You may give instructions, and the job may seem obvious to you, but it may not be to the team. If they don't know the steps to execute the plan, tasks may not get done. If someone gets angry, you now have a bigger problem.

Each individual needs to know what we want, what it looks like, how to do it, and why it's important. Then we need them to teach it back to us or have them teach it to another person. Teaching is only possible through comprehension. So instead of becoming frustrated when people are not doing the right thing, embrace the idea that they need more education.

Training is not just about telling, but starts with showing, and then repeating back, and then teaching it to someone else while we observe. It's like the old saying from medical training, "See one, do one, teach one."

What you're doing here is creating a space for executive work. Executive work means work done by a person's brain to plan and organize other work. Something like creating a new protocol, organizing workspace, or creating a project plan would be "executive." Such work is hard to do for some people. Others can do it, but not on demand in response to a specific situation. Others do it naturally, all the time.

Certain jobs get in the way of executive work. Assembly-line work, for example, is quite different from strategic thinking. If you take someone accustomed to such work, put them into a conference room, and ask them to think strategically, they could probably do it, but it might take some time to learn. Even if they knew how to do it, there might be a transition period in which they would have to change their way of thinking.

Many workers also are reluctant to engage in executive thinking. They worry they might make a mistake, or that their boss will think them presumptuous.

If you see your team not doing what they should be doing, it might be they need a bit of executive thinking applied to make the path clear. They might need a protocol to follow or permission to do some creative problem-solving. Or they might need you to make your expectations concrete, so that the path forward is clear.

Take the Time to Explain

While rounding in the hospital, occasionally a medical student will do a poor job of presenting a patient to the team. They will either omit data or present it in a confusing manner. For this situation, I have a single piece of paper I give them. It has little boxes on it with an outline of everything they need to gather. I say, "Go get all the information in these little boxes, and when you present the case, tell it to us with all the information in the order on the page." This solves the problem immediately.

–Mike

One of the strangest things I have seen in the workplace is leaders assuming that their reports will effortlessly know what to do, how to do it, why it's important, and how to correct it when things go wrong. These leaders believe they are giving clear direction but don't check to see if everyone understands. Then they get frustrated when their expectations are not met.

I saw this firsthand with a group of doctors who were required to switch to electronic records. Every doctor was given a tablet and expected to fill out a chart after seeing every patient. One doctor was not on board. He had been spoken to on multiple occasions. His coworkers were describing him as difficult and belligerent.

I went in and sat with him to see what was going on. After a few minutes, he sheepishly admitted he didn't understand the program, didn't know how to use the tablet, and was way out of his comfort zone with the changes. To replace this one doctor would have cost the group $250,000. No one had thought to ask if he needed help!

We were able to arrange for one of the office workers to spend a week shadowing the doctor, patiently showing him how to enter data, and helping when the system locked up. After that week, the problem was resolved.

When things aren't right, take a breath, check to see if the person really understands what is being asked, and ensure understanding. Getting frustrated and demanding more has no value if the person can't do what is being asked or doesn't understand what is needed.

–Joe

Moving Beyond the Natural

Step 1: Question some of the assumptions you might have made with your team.

Step 2: Ask yourself whether there is a better way you could train your team so they are better equipped.

Step 3: Write down two or three ways you can provide better clarity for your team.

Notes

Maxim 44

BAD FIT DOESN'T MAKE BAD PEOPLE

In recruiting and onboarding, most organizations emphasize the importance of their vision, values, mission, and culture. At the same time, it's very difficult to know up front if someone will fit once inside the organization. When the fit works, we often don't even notice or credit our own wisdom. But sometimes it doesn't work.

Bad fits are common. Sometimes, we find that we rushed the hiring process and didn't do our due diligence. We discover the individual oversold their abilities. Sometimes we find an individual's skills, styles, and needs clash with the workplace.

For example, a new hire may be very innovative but find themselves in an organization not looking to change course. A hire may be accustomed to a certain amount of decision-making authority that is just not possible in the new position.

The risk from a bad hire is actually greater for the individual than for the organization. The organization can always find a new person, but the individual who came in from the outside is depending on this organization for their livelihood.

The risk from a bad hire is actually greater for the individual than for the organization.

It's tempting to conclude that the new hire must have been a bad person or that the organization is bad. Neither is necessarily true.

When a bad fit is apparent, the employer should ask the following:

- Have we clearly articulated expectations and culture?
- Are we adequately engaged in helping this person be successful?
- Have we honestly discussed our specific concerns?

Likewise, the employee should ask the following:

- Is this a true clash of values, or just a clash of my personal preferences?
- Am I taking the time to learn the systems and procedures to see how they might work, rather than bypassing or ignoring them?
- Am I asking for help?

At the end of the day, understand that you are unique, just as each organization is unique. When the fit is off, embrace the positive in the individual, the boss, and the organization. Be thankful for the difference in each of us. See what you can do with those differences.

Good People Can Be Bad Fits

In an organization I was invited to work with, in a relatively short period of time I recognized that the leadership team had an unhealthy culture of talking about and laughing about people who had left. They labeled these folks as lazy, not smart, people who didn't care, and untalented.

As I got to know the group, what I found out was, as people left or were asked to leave, they were almost always demonized. They were referred to as bad people. This type of behavior and mindset is very unhealthy. People are people, they come and go, and we all fit some places but not others.

A key to healthy leadership is to focus on the fit, define the fit, and clarify what is necessary to be a fit on the team. When we do this, we not only set boundaries and show respect, but we give people the best chance possible to explore the workplace. Where the fit does not work for many possible reasons, the question is how we show respect, and honor the bad fit while still showing respect and dignity to the individual. The bottom line is the risk is always greater on the employees' end when they leave one organization and come and join your team. Employees often turn their lives and the lives of their families upside down to relocate and take a chance on your organization. If the fit is bad, the workplace typically just brings in someone else and continues to move forward. It is harder for the individual who thought they were a good

Good people are sometimes bad fits.

fit and later understood the fit was not as expected. This is just one of many reasons respect and understanding is important. Good people are sometimes bad fits. Never turn good people with bad fits into bad people, as you only add insult to injury.

–Joe

I'm not a bad person, but I wasn't that good as a journalist, which was my first career choice. Things other reporters found easy I struggled with. Small talk was tough. I couldn't approach strangers and get them talking. And approaching someone famous for a quote was nearly impossible. It just wasn't a good fit, and I left the field. But as Shakespeare said, "Sweet are the uses of adversity." The work changed me from a pure introvert into someone much more comfortable talking with others. And rapid writing is now easy.

–Mike

Moving Beyond the Natural

Step 1: Evaluate some great fits and misfits you have had along your hiring journey.

Step 2: Consider the differences. Why did one hire work out while another one failed?

Step 3: Take note of the people on your team today. Is there a bad fit? If so, what will you do to address this challenge?

Notes

Maxim 45

THE DIRECTION IS ALWAYS FORWARD

As a leader, you must pick the direction and decide where your group or organization is heading. That can be scary because choices have consequences. But remember, leaders are paid to do the hard stuff.

Advisors and boards can help. Research and the process of due diligence can help. You can get a team together to discuss it. Sooner or later, though, you must choose the direction. As you do, there are a couple points to keep in mind.

The Direction Is Always Forward

Leadership is always about moving people into the future. It is the leader's job to scope out that future state and then have the courage to move people toward the unknown. Then, they must move toward this new objective with confidence, not because they know they are right, because they don't. Rather, confidence for a leader comes because they know their team will adjust and adapt to whatever comes.

Doing nothing is not leading, and going back to the previous state is not leading. In the words of Martin Luther King Jr., "If you can't fly, then run; if you can't run, then walk; if you can't walk, then crawl. But whatever you do, you have to keep moving forward."

Leadership is always about moving people into the future.

This happens over and over. A company brings in a new CEO or division leader. They make some changes and fail. Now the organization brings back the old leader, who undoes the changes and brings the organization back to where it was. During these transitions, everyone tends to forget why the change was needed in the first place.

Forward is the only direction. To go backward is confused thinking and leads to failure.

You're Going to Bump into Something

If you run into an obstacle, find a way around. If it's an opportunity, seize it. Either way, learn from it.

A common element among successful innovators is that they were not looking for what they found. Dr. Alexander Fleming noticed that some mold on his culture dishes was inhibiting the growth of bacteria. This led to the creation of penicillin. "When I woke up just after dawn on September 28, 1928, I certainly didn't plan to revolutionize all medicine by discovering the world's first antibiotic," he wrote.

Think about your own life. What unforeseen obstacles have you bumped into? Who have you met? How have your plans changed? What opportunities did you find that you didn't even know existed? Who needs what you have to offer? How can your organization's strengths help others? When you are moving forward, these are the things that happen.

Plans are great, but reality is more complicated. Watch reality and be ready to change the plan.

You Never Know Where You Might End Up

I love traveling on a motorcycle. I never have plans, but I'm on the move. You never know how the weather, daylight, or unforeseen obstacles might play out. So you simply move in a direction with an idea in mind and see what you bump into along the way.

Recently, my wife and I were riding in Europe with dear friends. We left Spain and the Basque region and found ourselves in France. A few hours later, we stumbled across the Hotel Arce in a little town called Baigorri. The inn was owned by the fifth generation of a family. It was amazing.

Moving forward, you don't know where you will end up, but you will certainly bump into something along the way that is memorable. What a great way to travel through life, even if you don't want to do it on a motorcycle.

–Joe

I left journalism in 1989 because I couldn't handle it. I'm too much of an introvert. Shortly afterward I moved to Buffalo with my girlfriend (now my wife). She wanted to get a master's degree, and I didn't have anything better to do. When we arrived, I needed a job. I responded to a classified ad in the newspaper (that used to be a reasonable way to find work) and got a job as a secretary at a health insurance company. I figured, what the heck, I need a job, and I might learn something. And I really did learn. By accident, I had stumbled into a highly idealistic, progressive company that was one of the nation's first health maintenance organizations. The people I met there changed my life by showing me how the design of the system affects the care delivered. That insight provided the inspiration for my whole career.

–Mike

Moving Beyond the Natural

Step 1: Ask yourself, What is the hardest part of moving forward through seasons of adversity?

Step 2: Write down two to three obstacles you face today.

Step 3: Mentally prepare yourself to make adjustments.

Notes

Maxim 46

MOVE FROM TACTICAL TO EXPLORATORY CONVERSATIONS

Whenever people are together—in a work group, business partnership, campaign, religious institution, marriage, or even a group of friends—there are communication issues. The moment you take communication for granted is the moment it starts to decay.

Texting and social media make communication worse by giving the illusion of closeness and meaning. When used as a substitute for true communication, they make people more isolated and disconnected. As we write this, loneliness is at a high in the United States, and many feel their relationships are not meaningful. To get the best out of our teams, especially in situations where teams are working remotely, we must address isolation and loneliness. People need to feel seen and understood. The answer is to create good communication by moving from tactical to exploratory conversations.

Most interactions are tactical, dealing with practical, everyday concerns such as who, what, and where. They would easily fit into a text message, like "Where are we meeting for lunch today?" or "Running late," or "Will you call the customer about the report?" It's worthwhile reflecting on your own communication to see how much is just tactical.

Exploratory communication, on the other hand, involves asking questions. It goes beyond the immediate concerns and can allow conversations to become connections. People feel more valued and engaged. And at home, this kind of communication increases life satisfaction.

From Tactical to Exploratory

Here's an example of a conversation moving from tactical to exploratory:

Ann: Were you able to get the report done for the board?

Jim: Yes, I emailed it to you just a few minutes ago. Let me know if you have any questions.

Ann: You know, I have some questions right now. I'd be curious to know what stood out to you most as you put the report together.

Jim: I guess what stood out most is that our sales volume has been flat for quite a while.

Ann: What's your guess on why things are flat?

Jim: I think our market conditions are changing, along with the competition. Competition seems to be doing a few things that are giving them an advantage.

Ann: And how does that make you feel?

Jim: You know, it causes me a little bit of anxiety, as I look ahead. I wonder what will happen if the line remains flat or begins to go down.

Ann: If you were in my role, what would you do at this point, seeing what you see?

Jim: I'd get four or five of us together for a brainstorming session. We could hear from everybody about what they see and what their concerns are. We could move into wild ideas and suggestions, to see if there's anything that might make sense to try.

Ann: And what do you think this would do for us overall?

Jim: You know, I think it would help us feel more like a team and more active in our own future. This would make us feel like we were part of a solution, and we'd feel more important to you.

Ann: How would you feel about organizing the meeting and sending me an invite? Let's make it happen.

Jim: Really? That would be exciting. Thank you for trusting me to put this together.

If the conversation had stayed strictly tactical, Ann would have received the report and delivered it to the board, hoping the directors didn't ask too many questions. Jim, not hearing any concern from Ann about the company's competitive position, might start putting out feelers for a new position elsewhere. Moving the conversation to exploratory allowed for an enhanced connection. The interaction created vulnerability and transparency, which led to a stronger connection. As a bonus, if the board questions the report, Ann can now let them know what steps are already being taken.

How can this be applied to home life? An example is the challenge of raising teenagers. Many adolescents are reluctant to engage, and their parents frequently blame them for being reluctant to open up. But what if parents took more time to consider how much of their own side of these interactions was only tactical? Exploratory communication might not fix the relationship instantly, but it would be more likely to convince teenagers their parents care and are listening.

Start with something simple. For instance, instead of starting with an accusatory statement, such as "Why are you wearing that?"

try "That's a really interesting shirt. Where were you able to find that?" or "What is it about that shirt that caught your eye? What does that shirt say about you that you want the world to know?"

Moving Beyond the Natural

Step 1: Note some ways you might tend to take communication for granted.

Step 2: Consider a situation you face at work today and ask yourself how you could shift the conversation from tactical to exploratory.

Step 3: Write down two to three ways you could implement this strategy at home.

Notes

Maxim 47

VISION IS ABOUT LONG-TERM SERVICE TO HUMANITY

What's your vision? It's worth putting time and thought into developing a vision for lasting achievement of your own dreams and goals. In a well-run organization, there are opportunities for team members to achieve at least some piece of their own visions while contributing to something larger than themselves.

A vision is a mental picture of the future. The clearer the vision, the better. It can be either something that comes to you in a flash of inspiration or a mental picture you take years to construct, bit by bit. It should be exciting and easy to communicate to others.

No one can tell you what your vision should be, but here are some points to consider.

Think Long Term

Build a business you could work at for the rest of your career. There is excitement at the beginning. Running a start-up is energizing and can be full of victories. What would you create that would leave you still excited and proud in twenty years? What would you spend more time on, and what would you be more patient with, if the people, the systems, and the reputation would be around for that long? Think about the next generation. What if your child or another younger family member took it over? What would you be teaching your children about work ethic and professionalism?

Think About Serving Others

Consider what it would take to make a business that made people better, enriched the lives of others, and improved the world. It is not acceptable to ignore the impact your business has on people, their families, and the world. It can be natural to ignore these things, but leadership is about rising above those instincts.

Think About What You Allow

Whatever is happening is happening because you allow it. If you don't like what's going on, ask yourself why you allow it to take place. Do you have teams not hitting their deadlines? Ask yourself, *Why do I allow that?* Likewise, abusive behavior, dysfunctional meetings, or an antiquated software product. As psychologist Dr. Henry Cloud says, you are ridiculously in charge.

It doesn't matter if you have direct, formal authority over the matter in question. Your rank or salary does not matter. Leaders show up with what they have, no matter where they are. They have the willingness to stand up, ask questions, and keep asking those questions. They articulate a need, hold fast to it, and hold people accountable. They are not victims.

There is a certain faith you must have as a leader. You need faith that you can change things, that you can influence others, and that you can guide people around you toward what is right. Someone must take on this role, and deciding that you are the right person takes a kind of faith. Frequently, that faith must be embraced without clear evidence.

You Are in Charge of the Vision

In their third year, medical students rotate through the hospital, getting practical experience. A faculty member once said, "The students I get at the beginning of the third year look like second-year students. The students I get at the end of the third year look like doctors." Part of this transformation is that they are stepping up to the role of leader.

I ask students, "Who is in charge here? Who is the locus of order? It's you. You are the person who makes order out of chaos. You are the person who is thinking. You are the person who is responsible for outcomes. That's the essential function you are taking on." They listen, and they change. It's a different role than sitting in a lecture hall absorbing information or studying a cadaver in the gross anatomy lab. It's work, and it's the work of a leader.

–Mike

Years ago, I was speaking with an individual who created a pizza company. We were talking about vision, how his vision had changed significantly early on, and how this change impacted the way his company grew. He said, "Early on, I had a vision of people wrapped around the building waiting to pick up a pizza. However, before long the vision shifted. I still had a line of people wrapped around the building, but this time they were waiting in line to pick up a job application." He started to focus on culture rather than sales.

–Joe

Moving Beyond the Natural

Step 1: Write down a list of several values that are nonnegotiables in your life.

Step 2: Ask yourself, What am I contributing to the service of humanity?

Step 3: Take note of some things you allow today that need to be changed in the future.

Notes

Maxim 48

ACT ON THE OBVIOUS, AND YOU CAN CHANGE THE WORLD

The closer we are to something, the less clearly we see it. At work, standard procedures and daily routines do not attract our attention. We rarely stop and question the fundamentals or look for better ways to do things. When something works, we have little motivation to examine and change it.

There are no *best* procedures and routines, only better and better ones. The work you are doing now without thinking can always be improved. In fact, your current work may not be based on current knowledge and technology.

One way to reach breakthroughs is to grant permission for new hires to challenge you. They are looking at your old patterns with fresh eyes. Listen to them. What they say will give you insight into your assumptions. It will allow you to question what you thought were facts. When a new person asks questions, don't say, "It will make sense when you have been here longer," or "You'll see when you understand it better." By saying those things, you are pushing away important insights. Those questions are valuable.

It's unfortunate, but we all have confirmation bias. We look for data to support our belief that the way we are doing something is right. We push away contradicting data. So be smarter than this. Identify and acknowledge your assumptions and biases. Once you have found them, actively look for data that contradicts them. Anything you think is true will have much data to support it and minimal data to refute it. If there is reliable data that refutes your assumption, it means you do not understand the situation well enough.

As you are assessing a problem, stop yourself, look at all the data you have, and ask, "What here doesn't fit the pattern? What is the piece of information that is surprising? What makes me uncomfortable?" That information may lead you to an insight, or at least a new hypothesis about what is going on in your environment.

Another way to find an assumption or bias is to watch for your emotional reaction while reading or listening. When you read something uncomfortable and frightening, that's a clue it holds a lesson. So stop and think about it. True learning is not necessarily a comfortable process. If during your process of learning you always feel safe, you are not doing it right. Your assumptions and biases give you comfort, and looking into the unknown, and finding new things, can be quite uncomfortable.

When you read something uncomfortable and frightening, that's a clue it holds a lesson.

We need to be open to reviewing and challenging the assumptions we're working from, rather than working with a confirmation bias.

Never Stop Asking the Basic Questions

I like to tell medical students there are no "stupid questions," only basic ones. When you're on rounds in the hospital, the most basic question is sometimes, "Why is this patient in the hospital?" That question leads you to analyze the entire situation in terms of what the barriers are to discharge. In particular, it is useful when the patient has a constellation of unrelated severe problems, or an unclear problem. What do I have to do to get this patient home? Generally, this involves getting them disconnected from equipment, eating, and walking.

–Mike

Back in the early 2000s, we were working with a large textile organization. With this company a product was created in one plant, loaded onto a truck, and shipped to another plant where another piece of the process took place. As the company was looking to streamline costs and increase efficiency, we were shocked to find out that people in the first plant had never sat down with people in the second. When asked why we would suggest such a meeting, we replied, "It just seems to make sense. Let's see what comes of it."

When the groups got together, we started with a simple question: "What could we do on our end to make the product easier to handle and more ready for you on your end?" The results were astonishing! The two teams collaborated to reduce costs, gain efficiencies, and build cooperation. By doing nothing more than focusing on the obvious, a person can change the world (or at least their world).

Time and time again, executives will smile that little smile, say thanks, and then comment, "I can't believe we needed to bring someone in for something so obvious."

–Joe

Moving Beyond the Natural

Step 1: Invite some of the newer members on your team to share their feedback.

Step 2: Question some of the basic steps of your business. How could these be done more efficiently to better serve your customers?

Step 3: Never stop asking basic questions.

Notes

Maxim 49

HELP PEOPLE THRIVE

The best workplaces create space for employees to grow and develop. When people thrive, they create an energy that supports success. Getting employees to thrive is an art. Here are some important factors that are sometimes ignored.

Clarity of Expectations

Some people enter the workplace with realistic expectations, but many do not. For example, a new employee may expect to be promoted within their first year. It's important the leader clarifies expectations such as what the job entails, what success looks like, and what happens if the employee gets off course. Can the employee make decisions on their own, or should decisions be sent upward? Can employees hire people to build out their team based on what they believe they need, or is this handled by other people?

Trust and Respect

This sounds simple, but most of the time it's not. Trust in the workplace starts with the leader immediately and summarily trusting the employee. If the leader waits for employees to earn their trust, it creates a negative feedback loop in which people are never able to succeed.

The Ability to Speak Out

This is rare in an organization but highly useful. People need a way to speak out and share what they think doesn't make sense. When we bring in talented people, we need to give them permission to challenge the status quo, challenge our thinking, and challenge our decision-making in a way that is not threatening or negative but energizing and healthy. There must be an expectation that everyone will help each other get better. The opposite of that climate is hearing things like "I can't tell that to my boss."

A Guide to the Culture

Every workplace has unspoken rules, and we need to give people a guide to navigating them. Some of these rules are silly, like around what goes in the refrigerator, or who has unique use of what printer. This is all best handled through mentoring.

Regular Feedback and Coaching

These times need to be integral to the flow of the week, so it doesn't create anxiety or stress. When feedback and coaching are regular, and when they include commendations as well as criticisms, people will start to believe the organization is there to help them succeed.

Freedom to Enjoy Their Vacation

Self-care is counterintuitive to the flow of the workplace. Taking time and energy for ourselves can appear to be taking time and energy away from the organization. But people who work twelve hours are not more effective than people who work eight. And it's not good to avoid vacations.

Unfortunately, there is much pressure to spend time away from work, thinking about work, and doing work. Email and cell phones have allowed there to be no true separation when the day is over, or during vacation. It's not productive. The only antidote is for you, as a leader, to enforce the boundary between home and work. A CEO of a medium-size organization once said it well: "I hear people say they can't take their vacation. That's nonsense. If you don't take time to take care of you, how can you take care of your people and the organization?"

When you're on vacation, model good behavior. If you send emails on a day off or after hours, what does that tell your team about their time off? Is that good for them?

Set Clear Expectations

Recently, I was working with an organization that had experienced rapid growth, had a large footprint, and was exceeding financial expectations. Along with this, they also had a high turnover rate among the workforce and executives. When I started, a vice president had left after less than a year. This person was the sixth person in five years in that role.

In talking with the team, it became apparent that while financial opportunity drew people into the organization, a failure to have a plan to help people thrive led to a continual revolving door. They were doing everything wrong: There were no clear expectations. The job in question was basically impossible to do, given the resources and support available. There were disrespectful, personal attacks. There was no value placed on vacations and time off. We went over how all these things needed to change. It will be extremely difficult for this intense and financially driven team. However, if the change is not successfully made, their hopes for the future will not be achieved as the turnover, and low morale will continue.

–Joe

Much of American medical education revolves around seeing as many patients as possible. This pattern became popular after a leading doctor developed the grueling call system. He was a cocaine user. So basically, a young doctor who is on call every third night is following in the steps of a cocaine addict. This is not a healthy environment. It has taken medicine many decades to move into a better system.

–Mike

Moving Beyond the Natural

Step 1: Note some of the ways you create space for your employees to grow and develop.

Step 2: Ask yourself, Have I created a safe place for workers to share their thoughts?

Step 3: Evaluate the way you model self-care. Do you send emails when you shouldn't? Do you work too long? Do you set expectations of which few on your team can meet?

Notes

Maxim 50

DON'T GROW OLD WAITING FOR AN APOLOGY

When we feel we have been wronged, it's normal to want an apology. We want an acknowledgment of the wrong from the person we feel has wronged us. If we receive a sincere apology, it helps everything feel right. If we do not, it can lead to a grudge. Our thinking focuses on the person we feel has wronged us, and our relationship with that person can deteriorate, along with communication. Frequently, we will seek retaliation. Our behavior now no longer serves us or the organization. Our grudge is maladaptive.

For a leader, though, being personally right or wrong is not as important as moving forward to achieve goals with our team.

Part of our need for apologies is our drive to be right and to be seen as right. For a leader, though, being personally right or wrong is not as important as moving forward to achieve goals with our team. When we focus on a past hurt, slight, or mistake, we are abdicating part of our responsibility as leaders. Leadership is about teams and tomorrow, and not about self and yesterday.

Have Lunch with the Person Who Annoys You

All of us have someone in our work group who we are uncomfortable with or who rubs us the wrong way. Our natural inclination is either to oppose such people or avoid them. But leadership is overcoming the natural. So ask that person to lunch.

Why? Because it's bad for the organization to have tension between individuals who need to cooperate. Tension means communication and collaboration are not working at their finest. These people may avoid interaction when it's important.

It's not good to have anything like an enemy in your environment, especially someone you are stuck with. It's bad for your health, and it's bad for your ability to get things done. Make the enemy into a friend. Look for the good in this person, whatever it might be, and look for something you both care about.

This should be done over lunch. There is something magical about sharing a meal together that brings spirits closer. It's something basic to being human.

Sometimes You See Life from a Different Vantage Point

When I was in my early thirties, I was building a church congregation in North Carolina. In rapid succession we started to grow, added services, and began to relocate our facility. I had a vision for what we could do and had very little tolerance for those who wanted to interrupt the vision with facts. (I am not proud of that statement, but it is true.) People in the congregation who knew how to plan, build, and finance were not given the platform and respect they deserved. In all honesty, I thought they just didn't get it. However, what I came to learn was that what they saw, I couldn't see, and what I saw, they couldn't see. It was only when we brought together the two points of view that the congregation became successful and stable. I needed to embrace and learn from different points of view, instead of dismissing them.

–Joe

The person who annoys you is exactly the person who is exhibiting the characteristics you dislike and work against in yourself . Here is an interesting exercise for your private spiritual discipline: Identify one of these people, and list the specific points about them that annoy you. Next, forgive the other person for their flaws, and then watch for and forgive those same shortcomings in yourself. This will make you a better person.

–Mike

Moving Beyond the Natural

Step 1: Think of an area where you have been wronged.

Step 2: List some of the expectations you have for ways you think the other person could resolve this wrong.

Step 3: Rather than demand an apology, set up a lunch appointment with a person who annoys or has wronged you.

Notes

NOTES

Maxim 51

DON'T STEP ON OTHER PEOPLE'S VALUES

Values are the good things we move toward. Some of the points we might value include helping others, financial success, having political power, caring for animals, being well educated, having a happy marriage, working on interesting problems, supporting our children, or spending time with friends.

There are so many possibilities, and we can't move toward them all. We have limits to our time and energy, so we pick the ones that add the most meaning and purpose to our lives. Each of us has consciously or unconsciously chosen a set of them and acts on them. The action part is important. You can say you value exercise, but if you don't do it, it's not really that important.

When you become a leader, your values will be on display. Along with your vision and style, they will percolate through the organization. Your values will likely be seen as important for everyone. Organizations pick up the traits of their leaders. This is just human nature. The problem is the risk that your values will push aside everyone else's. That means you could be pushing aside the things that motivate your teams.

If a leader holds achievement as a value, this might translate into a competitive spirit among the staff. This spirit might result in lower priority being ascribed to collaboration and helping others. When this happens, the altruistic person doesn't feel like a team member, and this all looks like greed and toxic ambition to them. Do you want to lose this type of person?

Another reason to respect others' values is that teams sometimes expel leaders who do not. The people around you may see your values overtaking their own and decide you are not a good fit for the organization. After all, they, not you, will decide if you are successful.

We must allow people with a variety of values to feel comfortable. As in so many things, it's a question of balance. Each of us should see our chosen values as important while acknowledging and respecting others who have different choices. Someone who values independence, for example, should not have the right to step on people with a strong sense of interdependence.

The clearer values become, and the more we act on them, the more fulfilled we tend to be.

To understand your team's values, just talk to them about what they think is important. What are their priorities and goals? Why are they doing what they are doing? What gives them fulfillment and joy? What makes them operate in their "zone"? And what really puts them off or causes discord in their eyes? Another answer is to use a formal tool, such as the one at lifevaluesinventory.org by Dr. Kelly Crace.

The clearer values become, and the more we act on them, the more fulfilled we tend to be.

Understanding Comes through Communication

I was working with a large insurance company that had a major conflict brewing between three directors who ran three different divisions. For whatever reason these directors were viewed by others as competing with, disrespecting, and disliking one another. After a morning of meeting with the three of them, discussing the impact their relationship was having on the organization and on their own lives, they were asked to go have a two-hour lunch and get reacquainted with one another. Several people in the building saw them walking together to and from this event. On their return, they were laughing and smiling. The rumor mill went into overdrive with people trying to figure out what had happened. They never did become best friends, but they came to respect one another and work closely together without competition or defensiveness.

–Joe

We all have abrasive colleagues, people who rub others the wrong way. Many of these people will not change. Like all of us, they did not start life perfect, and they are not going to become perfect. When someone like this offends me, I tell them about it. I do this not because I expect an apology, but because if I don't tell them, I will just get angrier. I must clean off my own side of the street and leave what they do up to them.

–Mike

Moving Beyond the Natural

Step 1: List some of the ways your personal values might differ from those on your team.

Step 2: Write down some practical ways you could be more inclusive of other people's values.

Step 3: Commit to clear communication. If you have a problem to address, do not sit on it. Communicate with the other person and "clean off your own side of the street."

Notes

Maxim 52

REFLECTION IS A BETTER TEACHER THAN EXPERIENCE

To be effective, we must stop and reflect on what we are doing and how it affects the people around us. Reflecting is not merely thinking about *what* we did but on *why* we did it and how we were *feeling* and what we were *thinking*.

How could our actions have been more effective? Maybe we should have been questioning and listening instead of talking. Maybe we should have walked away without saying what we really meant. Maybe we should have waited before sharing the answer we knew, so that someone else who knew the answer could shine.

Reflecting includes considering others' reactions to something we have said or done. Was the other person staying engaged, or did they shut down and disconnect? Was the other person preoccupied? Was the other person seized with a different mindset or model, and how could we engage their perspective for better communication?

In the words of the ancient Greek playwright Menander, "People who do not reflect on their experiences are unpleasant." Reflection ensures we are tapping into our best thinking, rather than our natural thinking patterns. Reflection can help move us beyond our instincts into something better.

Why Reflection Is So Important

Often in my work with organizations, a key employee becomes disconnected and is fired. These moves often come as a shock. In hindsight, in most cases, the person had been given data, feedback, and coaching on multiple occasions. They almost always failed to reflect on the feedback and make the adjustments. Many times it takes these wake-up calls for people to stop, pause, reflect, and examine who they are, how they are working, how they are coming across, and what adjustments need to be made. The real challenge for a leader is how we find the opportunities for reflection before we fail.

–Joe

I was twenty-eight when I learned I had to pay more attention to how people reacted to me. I had taken a job in a health maintenance organization in Buffalo. A vice president had been watching me in meetings. One day he said, "You're really focused on contributing what you see as the truth. But you must pay attention to how people react to the things you say. You should pay attention to your wording, your timing, and the emotions you display."

> I started making it a habit to watch carefully when I say something to people. That's taught me a lot about how abrasive I can be.
>
> *–Mike*

Moving Beyond the Natural

Step 1: As this book comes to a close, carve out some time for personal self-reflection.

Step 2: After reading these fifty-two maxims, list some unnatural ways you could improve your leadership. Which one of these fifty-two resonated with you the most?

Step 3: Commit your life to continuous improvement. Remain a student and look for others to be your teachers.

Notes

Practicalities

CHOOSE A PATH TO DEVELOP YOURSELF

Developing yourself means learning, stretching yourself, and becoming more comfortable being uncomfortable. In choosing a path of self-development, we must consider how comfortable we are with taking risks. After all, not everyone is extraverted and assertive.

Path 1: The No-Risk Approach

This approach is the most basic and nonthreatening. You do not have to tell anyone what you're doing, and you don't have to ask anyone anything.

READ

This is a nonnegotiable necessity. Read books, read book synopses, or listen to audiobooks. Reading brings you outside yourself. Biographies are a great start. Move on to topics where you need to grow, like public speaking, conflict management, candor, strategy, or team dynamics. Reading is never a waste of time if we take a posture of learning. At worst, it validates what we already knew.

JOURNAL

Journaling has gotten lost today, mostly due to technology. Note that this is not keeping a diary. Journaling is a reflective process where we evaluate what we did, what our fear was while we were doing it, what we missed that is now clear, and what might be a better approach to the same issue next time. To journal on what we stumble over for twenty minutes three times a week brings clarity without any risk. Private reflection like this allows us to be more graceful in our professional lives.

CHOOSE A COMPETENCY AND GOOGLE IT

Find a list of competencies for the position you seek. Find the one that is the most difficult, frightening, or foreign. Google "developmental learning" around that competency and lay out a plan.

Path 2: The Moderate-Risk Approach

This takes a bit more intention. It includes others in your self-development journey by welcoming their feedback. These steps might include attending a professional educational opportunity at your local college or a workshop seminar.

FIND A MENTOR

Identify someone in your circle who does something you admire or respect, or has something you want, and develop a mentoring relationship. Figure out how you can spend more time with this individual to listen, observe, and ask questions without formal expectations. An obvious risk is the person you've identified might not respond, which could leave you with a sense of rejection. If that happens, identify the next person to approach. There is something we can learn from everyone.

MENTOR SOMEONE ELSE

Find someone who is struggling and invest your time and effort getting to know that individual, helping them to improve in whatever area they are looking to improve within your comfort and expertise. There are endless opportunities to do this on a community level. Mentoring forces us to clarify our thinking and our understanding as we work to help the other person.

ASK THE BIG QUESTIONS

Ask your boss or supervisor a single question once every six months. Here are some options: What is the competency you would like to see me improve on? What is it that gets in my own way of reaching my potential? What should I improve about the way I work?

Find someone in your team you're comfortable with and ask them periodically what you should be working on. This can be a coworker, a direct report, or a supervisor. The risk is moderate because you are opening yourself up to a response you don't control. These questions will probably just open up useful conversations.

Path 3: The Higher-Risk Approach

This approach requires you to be the most vulnerable, but it always promises the greatest return on your efforts. It might include engaging in a formalized mentoring program, at work or through an association. Ideally, the mentor should be assigned, the agenda laid out, and accountability expected. This is high risk because the mentor might not like you or vice versa.

Go to your supervisor or the HR department and ask them to run a 360-degree assessment. You will find out how you are doing in the eyes of your direct reports, peers, and supervisor. It's a higher risk because we're asking for information about our shortcomings. It can take a while to become comfortable with this kind of information.

Go back to school and engage in a formal program, usually a degree or certification. This is a higher risk because it disrupts your family system by taking up your time and energy, while you run the risk of investing time and money without a clear assurance that you'll be able to finish.

Ask These Questions of Everyone on Your Team

It's easy for relationships to move away from the genuine and become shallow and transactional. For example, at home, we may be discussing who must take the kids where and who needs to go to the store, but not how we feel or think about something. Shallow interactions make people feel invisible. They lead us to create stories around the behavior of others that have nothing to do with reality. Shallow relationships won't get us through tough times.

We need emotional attachments to the people we work with, and even more so to the people we live with. We strengthen our emotional attachments by knowing what the other person values and wants. Here are examples of a few questions that get to the heart of another person's values:

- Name the one person other than a parent who had the greatest influence on your life. In a word or two, what did they teach you?
- If you were to be described in three words, which would you most like to hear?
- If you could do anything at all with your life without harm to those you care about, what would you do?

Write the answers down. They are extremely useful. You can use the answer to the "three words" question to engage the individual better. You know them better, and you can manage them more easily, because you're not making up stories about them. You're not making assumptions about their character and what drives them.

Why do you need these answers for people in your house? Because they're more important than the people at work and should at least receive the same treatment.

Look for These Cognitive Biases in Yourself

Despite our culture being swamped with illusions and falsehoods, it's always important to understand what is true and real. That's not always easy, because each of us has mental limits. One powerful way to get past your mental limits is to carefully study your biases. It will make you better at what you do.

The art of thinking clearly has been studied for millennia and has left behind many crystalized lessons available in the world's culture. One set of lessons we have is a list of cognitive biases, which are classical ways that thinking is disrupted by irrationality, even in the best of us. Here are some examples:

- **Selection bias:** Your understanding of a situation is affected by the examples you examine, which are not representative of the whole. For example, if you choose a focus group of retired people, the ideas they generate about your product will be limited.
- **Anchoring:** In a negotiation, the first offer creates a framework for subsequent discussion. Also, the first option in a series of choices tends to set expectations.
- **Sunk cost fallacy:** When you've invested lots of time or money in a project, you are less likely to abandon it when it is failing. This is very powerful, because people don't like to admit they are wrong, so they won't admit something is failing.
- **Framing effect:** When you're approaching a problem, decisions or ideas made early on tend to affect work very far down the road—even to the extent of limiting the outcome. If we don't question the fundamentals regularly, early errors can continue.
- **Halo effect:** When you like someone for one talent, you tend to think they're good at other things too.
- **Out of sight, out of mind:** We tend not to think about people and things that are not immediately pressing on our attention. This is especially true for individuals or ideas that carry a negative emotional feeling.

- **Bandwagon effect:** You believe something because others believe it.
- **Recall bias:** People's memories of the past are affected by things that happened after the memory was formed.
- **Confirmation bias:** You tend to evaluate information in ways that support our existing opinions. People tend to hold on to their opinions despite contrary evidence.

Notes

Concluding Maxim

THE WORK OF DEVELOPMENT IS NEVER COMPLETE

This book is an attempt to see into the depths of the role of the leader, which is a fundamental and ancient element of our humanity.

In our view, leadership is rising above your natural instincts. It is the process of continually becoming your better self. Becoming a leader is a decision, and not necessarily the fulfillment of a natural inclination or a promotion. The hardest part about that decision is that it will change your life, and there are things, and maybe even people, that you will need to leave behind.

A key to success is to make your team more important than you. They should solve problems, they should shine, they should grow, and they should be able to replace you. And they, after all, determine whether you will be successful. Give them a safe environment where they can thrive.

Leadership requires self-reflection, leading to self-knowledge. Most essentially, that self-knowledge should focus on your own internal emotional landscape. You will never fully understand this landscape—there is always a shadow side, and if you don't acknowledge the shadow side, it's dangerous. You will reflect better, and know yourself better, if you develop relationships with a set of people who will give you honest feedback. This is especially important because at work, you will usually be the last person to know what people really think of you.

Self-understanding is hard, like many tasks that fall to a leader. But being hard doesn't make it wrong. Your job, in fact, is to do the hard things. For example, it's your job to handle conflict.

Ultimately the things you learn about yourself will be universal truths about you and your situations. And knowing those truths will make all aspects of your life better. Some of those things will make you quite uncomfortable. You will be tempted to look for answers to this discomfort at work—but don't do it; your workplace isn't the place to heal.

You will be anxious and afraid, but to be your best, you must experience these natural emotions and turn them into allies and tools to make you better. If you're not aware of your fear, and the distrust it creates, those emotions will sabotage you and make you fail.

You will be shown to be wrong sometimes, and it is important to embrace those times. After all, you don't know everything, and that's why you have a team.

People follow leaders who do the right thing, and doing the right thing is essential to every aspect of your job.

It's easy to fall into the trap of trying to please the people who can't be pleased. Instead, you should please the people around you whose work is critical to the organization's success.

To lead you must be listened to, and people listen to people who are competent, compassionate, and consistent. In turn, you must listen—and you listen best when you use everything you have learned about yourself through self-reflection. If you use emotional awareness while controlling your thoughts and stay rational, your feelings will ultimately follow along, like the wheels of a trailer behind a car.

It is essential to fight the natural inclination to stop thinking. It is natural to tell ourselves the same stories over and over, no matter how inaccurate they might be. This is one of the ways we deal with uncertainty, which is uncomfortable and hard to face. But if we use our curiosity and courage to investigate uncertainty, we can learn valuable lessons, some of which end up being obvious in hindsight.

Another approach to uncertainty is to accept there are many ways to approach a problem or a question. In real life there are many answers to a question. A great way to find different answers is to have a diversity of perspectives working on a problem.

Trust in an organization should start with you as the leader. Tell your team the truth about what you see, even if it's disruptive—perhaps especially then—because it's natural not to want to rock the boat.

Boundaries solve many problems. For example, they can solve the problem of a leader's loneliness without creating inappropriate side effects. One boundary we have found useful, but which likely appears cold, is one against having true friends at work, because it impairs organizational function and success. Another important boundary should be around letting others see it when you disagree with your boss. Part of your job is to make your boss look good. Be useful to your boss and the organization and find ways to make yourself more useful.

You need to understand your team. If you want to see who the best leader is in your team, it's likely the person who has gotten others promoted. If someone annoys you, get to know them especially well.

That said, not everyone will fit in your team. But that doesn't mean they are not good people.

When you're talking to them, ask open-ended questions and explore their understanding. Especially examine the things that underly their understanding and perspectives. What are their values? What is truly important to them?

Don't let your intelligence be a liability. Keep it focused on the good of the group and make sure you keep it scrupulously updated on reality, lest you start making castles in the clouds.

Your job is to move your team forward in the face of uncertainty, creating value for humanity in the long term.

As you read through these maxims and find yourself questioning how to incorporate them into your everyday routines and interactions, feel free to reach out and call either Mike or Joe. We'd be happy to discuss your situation with you.

ACKNOWLEDGMENTS

Both of us have sat at the feet of amazing people for years. Listing names doesn't seem right, because we would leave some off, and so many people shared their valuable wisdom with us. We are also grateful that they allowed us to share something with them, in turn.

Notes

Made in United States
North Haven, CT
23 May 2023

36896099R00243